Sir *ISAAC* NEWTON's

PHILOSOPHY

EXPLAIN'D

For the Use of the Ladies.

In Six Dialogues

on

LIGHT and COLOURS.

From the Italian of Sig. *Algarotti*.

VOLUME II.

Quæ legat ipsa Lycoris. Virg. Ec. x.

LONDON:
Printed for E. Cave at St *John's* Gate,
MDCCXXXIX.

The FOURTH DIALOGUE.

Encomium on Experimental Philosophy, and an Expoſition of the NEWTONIAN *Syſtem of Optics.*

THE next Day when we had diſengaged ourſelves from Poetry, which had at firſt given Birth to our Diſcourſes on Light and Colour, and afterwards endeavoured to diſturb and interrupt it, I began after the following Manner. It is now Time, Madam, to lead you into the moſt retired Sanctuary of Philoſophy, from whence the Profane and thoſe who are filled with Vortices, Globules, Atoms, ſubtile Matter, and like Imaginations are entirely excluded. This Philoſophy which I am now conducting you to, is leſs pompous than that we have already diſcourſed on, but in Return, performs all its Promiſes; a Philoſophy, which is contented with giving a Hiſtory of Phyſics, and leaves to others the Province of making them the Subject of a Romance. You have had an Inſtance of the one in its Method of explaining the Nature of Viſion, and the Syſtem of Vortices has given you an Example of the latter more pompous and ſplendid Philoſophy, which boldly goes to the firſt Cauſes of Things, and laying down certain arbitrary Principles, upon theſe builds the World, and explains all the Phænomena of it according to its own Fancy.

As the Eye is now diſcovered to have an entire Reſemblance to the artificial *Camera oſcura*, all Philoſophers will hereafter explain the Nature of Viſion after the ſame Manner. But there will not be that Conformity in their Opinions concerning the Solidity of Bodies, Gravity, Light, and Colours, ſince the Cauſe of theſe Qualities can be known only by Conjecture. And how very hazardous a Thing this is, you have already

ſeen

ſeen in the *Carteſian* Syſtem of Globules, to ſay nothing of *Mallebranche*'s Reformation, which, notwithſtanding all the Applauſes at firſt given it, is now exploded, and ſhares the ſame Fate as the Globules. And this you may believe has been the Caſe with all the general Syſtems that have hitherto appeared, concerning the Cauſes of Things. They reſemble vaſt Empires, which totter and fall by their own Weight and Greatneſs. I find then, ſaid the Marchioneſs, that the *wherefore*, which ſo greatly excites our Curioſity, will be for ever hid from us, and the Pleaſure of conjecturing, which is generally ſo adapted to the Taſte of *Men*, will have no Charms for *Philoſophers*. This really is a Circumſtance, which will make the Condition of thoſe Gentlemen not greatly to be envied by the Vulgar.

Conjecture (anſwer'd I) according to the Aſſertion of one of the moſt ingenious Authors in the World, is not to be allowed in any Thing but Geometry. In this Science, if the Certainty of

Principles does not directly guide us to what we ſeek, it never leads us however to any Thing contrary, and always rewards our Searches with ſomething equivalent. But what Uncertainty and and Inconſtancy is there in Natural Philoſophy? Some affirm that there is a Vacuum, or Space void of all Body, and others will have every Thing to be Body. This Diverſity of Opinions, with regard to Principles, muſt unavoidably produce very great and innumerable Diſputes as they advance further, which extend ſo far as the fixing the Eſſence or Nature of Body, a Thing which one would imagine ſhould of all others be the moſt certain in Phyſics, ſince Body and the Properties which depend on its Eſſence, are the perpetual Subject of Philoſophical Inquiries. I cannot help comparing theſe Philoſophers to thoſe Critical Writers who correct ſome corrupted and defective Paſſage of an ancient Author. One of theſe Gentlemen gives one Reading, a ſecond another, each ſupported with the fineſt

and

and moſt elaborate Arguments, and the Encomiums of the Journaliſts of the Learned. Some old Manuſcript of the Author himſelf at length appears drawn out from the Duſt and Obſcurity of a Library, and then all the fine Readings of theſe profound Critics, and the Time they ſpent in inventing them, are ſent into the Regions of *Arioſto*'s Moon, and are there treaſured up among other loſt Things. Obſervations and Experiments are the authentic and original Manuſcripts of Nature; and theſe, by overthrowing ſo many fine Syſtems, inſtruct us every Day, to be more cautious in puzzling ourſelves to form Hypotheſes. I look upon this Advice as a very great Benefit to Mankind, ſince it exempts them from no ſmall Trouble and Fatigue. But the Misfortune is, that Men perſiſt in a Refuſal of this friendly Admonition, and are obſtinately bent to ſpend their Time to no Purpoſe.

This is indeed a Practice that redounds greatly to the Honour of theſe *Obſervations* of yours (ſaid the Marchioneſs.)

chioness.) A System need only be ingenious, simple and elegant, to give them a Right to declare open War against it, they may be termed the *Erostratuses* of Natural Philosophy, which found their Glory in the Destruction of all that is grand and splendid. I must confess that I cannot be pleased with so malicious a Character. To what a Height would your Displeasure rise, answered I, if I had told you all that these Observations are capable of effecting. There is perhaps no System better grounded than this, that Animals have Wings given them in order to fly, and Legs to walk. And yet Observation has discovered to us certain Insects who have large Wings without ever making Use of them to fly with; and in the same Manner, there is one Animal, which, notwithstanding it has Legs disposed like those of others, formed in the same Manner and of the like Proportions, yet almost always walks upon its Back with its Legs upwards, just as if the first were not sensible they had Wings, nor the last,

laſt, Legs. It is true, however, that if Obſervations had done no greater Service to the World than to deſtroy, we ſhould not be much indebted to them. But by overthrowing perplexed and uſeleſs, and ſometimes very troubleſome Syſtems, how many good and uſeful Diſcoveries have theſe Obſervations furniſhed us with, in the Room of thoſe Hypotheſes they have overthrown?

Some melancholy Philoſophers have imagined the Rays of the Moon were cold and humid, and therefore greatly to be feared, ſince there muſt be expected very dangerous Effects from their Influence. And in fact you ſee many Perſons, even now, who believing the Effects of this Planet from the Tradition of their Fore-fathers, retire as ſoon as ever the Moon begins to riſe, and (as they expreſs it) gets Strength; and vaſt Numbers of People are perſwaded that they have the Head-ach, if by walking in the Evening they have unhappily been obliged to receive the Infection of its Light.

The Experiments which have been

made upon this, give us full Liberty to walk at what Hour we please, without apprehending any Danger from that Quarter. The Rays of this Planet collected in the Focus of a burning Glass or a Lens, do not cause any sensible Effect in the Bodies upon which they fall, notwithstanding they are sometimes two thousand Times denser when thus collected, than they ordinarily are. A Thermometre, which is an Instrument containing a Liquor that contracts with the least Cold, and dilates with the least Heat, does not suffer any Alteration in the Focus of these Glasses when they are exposed to the Rays of the Moon; whereas if they are exposed to those of the Sun, the Vehemence of their Heat surpasses that of the hottest Furnaces, so that the *Amiantus* which defended the precious Ashes of Antiquity from the devouring Flames of the funeral Pile, cannot defend itself from the violent Heat of these Glasses. The Rays of the Moon do not appear to have any other Quality than that of supplying the Absence of the Sun, and inspi-

inſpiring a ſoft and pleaſing Melancholy in the Hearts of Lovers.

Theſe Sorts of Obſervations, ſaid the Marchioneſs, I have no Objection to, which let the fine Syſtems alone, and deliver Mankind from ill-grounded Fears. To this Spirit of Obſervation, anſwered I, we are indebted for our Deliverance from other much more important Fears, Comets, Pillars of Fire, Showers of Blood, and *Ignes fatui*, anciently Marks of Divine Wrath, do not at preſent diſturb ſo much as one half Hour's Sleep, except it be in thoſe Perſons who will always be the *Vulgar*, and always of a Temper fitted to receive theſe Impreſſions of Terror from others.

But how much are we indebted to the Study of Experiments! Aſtronomy, Natural Hiſtory, and Anatomy, ſeem by the Aſſiſtance of this to be rather new Sciences born among the Moderns, than tranſmitted from the Ancients to us. To this Anatomy owes the Circulation of the Blood, and all the animal OEconomy, whoſe very Simplicity was the

the Cauſe of its being ſo little known among the Ancients. To this, Chemiſtry is obliged for its Phoſphorus: Aſtronomy, for its exact Predictions: Hydroſtatics, for an eaſy Method of Living, and carrying freſh Air for Reſpiration, in an Element denied to Men: for Acouſtics, and their ſpeaking Trumpet; their Projects, for rendering the Perfection of Hearing equal to that of Sight, and innumerable muſical Inſtruments, the Offſpring of Harmony. To this, Optics owe their Teleſcopes, Microſcopes, Magic Lanthorns, and an infinite Number of other Wonders that perfect or flatter the Senſe of Seeing.

Superſtition, Credulity, and a greater Love for the Marvellous, than Truth, Negligence, and a Want of proper Means for Obſervation, have for a long time been inſuperable Obſtacles to Knowledge. How great a Treaſure of Wonders has Natural Hiſtory, after having rejected the Abſurdities of the Ancients, demonſtrated to us! New Modes of Production, Breathing, Seeing and Living, new Conformation of Parts, new

new Societies, new Modes of Being, unheard and unknown to paſt Ages.

The Reaſon of Mankind has been poliſhed in Proportion as that of Brutes has been more conſidered; and the Arts themſelves have been brought to Perfection by Obſervation upon certain Animals, commonly regarded either with Horror, or as the Refuſe of Nature. Spiders have furniſhed our Manufactures with new Species of Silks; and the Eggs of a Fiſh, tho' yet unknown, may, with a little Apparatus, give us a fine purple Colour not inferior to that ſo much celebrated by the Ancients. Shall I inform you of the Experiments made concerning the Weight of Air, and the Power it has of dilating itſelf when compreſſed; Experiments once termed the Wonders of *Magdebourg*? Shall I give you an Account of the Equilibrium of Fluids, the Vegetation and Culture of Plants, which have afforded ſo great an Advantage and Ornament to Society? By theſe Experiments your Garden is embelliſhed with the playing and agreeable Murmur of arti-

artificial Fountains; and these supply the Northern Tables in great Plenty with those delicious Fruits that Nature had confined to a warmer Hemisphere. The Orange by these transported from the *China* to the *Portuguese* Soil, sweetly allays the burning Heat of the Summer; and these Experiments have extracted from the Vines. of the *Rhine* transplanted upon the burning Rocks of *Canary*, that agreeable Juice so pleasing to the Taste of Ladies. Still better and better, said the Marchioness. Is not this the Cluster of the promised Land by which you hope to allure me? and as we are in the Country, would intice me by the Hopes and Advantages which accrue from Observation to Agriculture and OEconomy? Without Dispute you have those ancient Consuls in your Head, who from the Triumph returned to the Culture of their Farms.

If I had a Design of inticing you, answered I, Madam, I should rather entertain you with talking of the polite Arts of which you are so fond, and which owe both their Origihal and Progress to Obser-

Obſervation and Imitation. Gratitude requires you to think yourſelf obliged to theſe for the Pleaſure you receive from the fine Lineaments and elegant Air of Countenance in the Meduſa of *Strozzi*, the juſt Gradation of the Anger of *Achilles*, the Variety and Strength of Paſſions in *Caſſandra*, that Maſter-piece of the *Timotheus* of our Age, the majeſtic Solidity of the Portico of the Rotunda, the elegant Strokes of *Guido*, and the magic Colouring of *Rubens*. What Riches has this induſtrious Philoſophy brought into the Treaſuries of Painting, by the Obſervation of ſo many new Animals and Plants? What an additional Beauty has it given by the Imitation of the Eaſtern Varniſh, to certain Works deſigned for the Uſe of thoſe People to whom Superfluity is neceſſary? What a fruitful Source of Similies and Deſcriptions has it by its new Diſcoveries opened to Poetry? The Sun, Stars, Shepherds, the *Hyrcanian* Tiger, and the like common place Compariſons, are delivered from the Weight which they

alone

alone have long borne in Poems, and we from the Fatigue of hearing them ſo often repeated. How great a Progreſs has the Elegance of Dreſs, which ſo greatly heightens the Beauties of Nature; and in ſhort, the moſt polite of all the Arts made in our Age, by the Aſſiſtance of a curious Obſervation made upon pleaſing Objects, Beauty itſelf, the moſt valuable Treaſure with which Nature can enrich and adorn Youth, would often be a vain and uſeleſs Gift, if Obſervation had not conſulted its Safety, by bringing in the ſtrange, yet ſalutary Art of furniſhing ourſelves with a particular Diſtemper whenever we pleaſe? How many fair *Circaſſians*, who formed for the Pleaſure of the Univerſe, are confined to a Seraglio, and ſubjected to the Caprices of one ſingle Tyrant, and how many Beauties in *England*, the Miſtreſſes of free born Hearts, owe their Empires and their Arms to an early Inoculation of the Small Pox?

But not to inſiſt on what you may poſſibly think I might acquire too great an Advantage from, nor to ſay any Thing further of Natural Philoſophy, which ſeems a Province the moſt adapted to the Diſcoveries of Obſervations, is not Policy indebted to *theſe* for that wiſe and real Government, which renders the Southern Suns leſs pleaſing than the Cloudy Regions of the North, where the Liberty of the People is made compatible with the Superiority of the Nobles, and the Authority of the Sovereign? Metaphyſics, that Labyrinth of Reaſon, are obliged to theſe for a certain Syſtem of the Origin and Progreſs of our Ideas, and we for the Knowledge of our ſelves. The Chaos of Chronology and Hiſtory has from theſe Obſervations received its Light and Order. Sir *Iſaac Newton*, that divine Philoſopher, who may be regarded as the Founder of human Knowledge, has from Obſervations drawn chiefly from the ordinary Courſe of Nature, ranged hiſtorical Facts in a certain Series, by joining Epochas, which the Ignorance or Pride of Mankind had ſet at a great Diſtance from

from each other, in the ſame Manner as a judicious Obſervation had united the Boundaries of the Earth in Geography.

Conducted by this infallible Guide he, according to the Expreſſion of one of his Countrymen,

Diſplay'd the lucid Robe of Day,

and thence extracted the true Properties of Light and Colours (which had till that Time lain concealed and involved) without forming, like *Des Cartes* and his Followers, any imaginary Syſtem to explain the Nature of them.

This is a World entirely new, enriched with the moſt ſhining Truths, and diſcover'd by *Newton* alone, for there are not the leaſt Traces of any Philoſopher who ever appear'd there before him. His Treatiſe of Optics, the Production of thirty Years Study and Search, is an excellent Model of true Philoſophy. One ſingle Experiment of his has advanced our Diſcoveries more than all the ingenious and magnificent Syſ-

Syſtems put together, that had ever gone before him.

An antique Column of the moſt worthleſs Stone has more Beauties in the Eyes of a Connoiſſeur, and will conduce more to the Perfection of Architecture than all the Galleries of Emerald and Adamant, invented by the Poets to adorn their inchanted Palaces.

But your Connoiſſeur, ſaid the Marchioneſs, cannot admire or taſte the Beauties of a Column, however antique and well-proportion'd it may be, unleſs he firſt knows what a Column is. And how is it poſſible that we ſhould underſtand the Properties of Light and Colour, as you tell me *Newton* does, without firſt fixing what the Colours themſelves are, and explaining the Nature of them? *Des Cartes*, whoſe Syſtem you Moderns explode, tells me, that if a Ray of Light meets with the ſolid Parts of a Body, it is repelled and reflected, and I underſtand this very well, becauſe he had before told me that a Ray of Light is nothing but a *String* of little Globules. But how can I ever underſtand the

the new Diſcoveries concerning the Qualities of Light, unleſs I am firſt informed what Light itſelf is?

Is there any Thing, anſwered I, more inexplicable than the Nature and Cauſes of muſcular Motion? All the Diſſertations of Philoſophers upon it have been in vain. (And indeed the more theſe diſpute upon the Cauſes of Things, the more inexplicable do they generally make them.) And yet an excellent Painter, a *Michael Angelo*, by laying down certain Rules drawn from repeated Obſervations, would have informed you, that when the Body makes ſuch a particular Motion or Effort, certain Muſcles muſt be elevated, and others lowered and depreſſed. So that there is no Poſture ſo ſtrange but he could have foretold the various and almoſt infinite Motions they would produce. The famous Piece of the laſt Judgment, in the Vatican, is an evident Proof of his Knowledge in this Point.

The Loadſtone is a Secret of the ſame Kind. Its Nature and the Cauſe of of its ſurprizing Effects are, and perhaps always will be as entirely loſt to Philoſophers as the *Punic* Language is to Critics.

Our Ignorance of its Cauſe, however, does not hinder us from making very many Diſcoveries of its Qualities. We know, for Inſtance, that if it be armed with Steel it can attract a much greater Quantity of Iron than it can unarmed. We have diſcover'd that on one Side it attracts another Loadſtone, and repels it on the other, and conſtantly directs itſelf to the Poles of the World. To this, Natural Philoſophy owes the Diſcovery of a great Number of Truths, to this Navigation its Compaſs, and Commerce and Mankind very many Advantages.

If it is ever poſſible to arrive at a Knowledge of the Nature of Things, this is the only Method, by obſerving and inveſtigating, with the greateſt Attention, their moſt ſecret and hidden Properties, their primitive and elementary Qualities, on which all the reſt depend.

Hi-

Hithertò you have ſeen only the different Modes of the human Imagination in thoſe Syſtems, continually changing and ſucceeding each other, to gratify the Pride of Man, that always deluded yet ſtill credulous Being. But at preſent Light and Truth itſelf addreſs you in the Language of Sir *Iſaac Newton.* Let us hearken to it attentively, ſaid the Marchioneſs. Let it diſſipate any Remains of Darkneſs, that may ſtill obſcure my Mind, and conduct me into this new World of Philoſophy.

I obſerv'd to you the other Day, anſwer'd I, that every Ray of Light, however ſlender, is nothing but a Collection of innumerable other Rays, which are not all of the ſame Colour, notwithſtanding the whole Ray appears white: But ſome of theſe Rays are red, orange, others yellow, green, blue, indigo, or violet, beſides innumerable Degrees of intermediate Colours between each of theſe ſeven principal Ones. Theſe Rays of different Colours, which are called *primary*

mary or *homogeneal*, blended together form a heterogeneous Compound Ray of a white or golden Colour, ſuch as a Ray of the Sun appears, juſt in the ſame Manner as different Colours mix'd together upon a Painter's Pallet, compoſe a new One, which has ſomething of all the others in general, but is different from each of them in particular. Theſe are the Reaſons why that Poet (whom you diſcovered rather from his Eſteem for you than by his Stile) in ſpeaking of Light, uſes the Expreſſion *golden* and *ſevenfold*, an Epithet anciently appropriated to the *Nile* and the Shields of Heroes. This *ſevenfold* Light is the inexhauſtible Treaſury of thoſe innumerable Colours, which form the gay Picture of the Univerſe, and its Rays are not tinged with the Purple or Sapphire, either when they are refracted through a Priſm, or reflected from a Surface, but derive their Colour from the Sun himſelf with that Heat and Luſtre, which they receive from him, tho' not diſcovered by Vulgar Eyes.

In ſhort, every Ray may be conſi-der'd as a Fibre compoſed of innume-rable other Fibres or Filaments, each of which has a peculiar, proper, and unchangeable Colour, which it would infallibly diſcover to our Eyes, if it could be ſeen, ſeparated from the other Colours, which concur with it in for-ming the white or yellowiſh Colour of Light. But how indefatigable muſt be the Induſtry of that Philoſopher, who could divide and reſolve the whole Ray into its primary and elementary Rays, ſo that every one of them ſhould ex-hibit its own Colour? It is certain this Diviſion could never happen if theſe primary and homogeneal Rays were not of ſuch a Nature that ſome are refracted more than others in paſſing all with the ſame Inclination out of one Medium into another, (from Air into Glaſs, for Example) and by this Means are diſunited and ſeparated from each other.

This Propoſition, that *Rays which differ in Colour differ alſo in Degrees of Refrangibility*, is the fundamental

Diſco-

Discovery, upon which the *Newtonian* System of Optics is built. Agreeably to this it is demonstated that the violet Rays are the most refrangible of all. Next follow the indigo, then the blue, green, yellow, orange, and lastly the red, which are the least broken of any by Refraction. Do I explain myself clearly enough, *Madam*, for you to conceive my Meaning?

Extremely well, answered she: I understand very easily, that Nature, by making Rays which are different in Colour, different likewise in Refrangibility, has furnished Philosophers with a Means of separating them, which otherwise would be impossible. The Properties of this Light which you have been describing, are indeed very surprizing. A Philosopher must have a very great and enterprizing Genius that could make such Discoveries; and his Credit ought to be supported by very weighty Arguments drawn from frequent Observations, which I must confess I am extremely impatient to be acquainted with. I who was at first a

Cartesian, afterwards a Disciple of *Mallebranche*, now find myself without any System at all. This is a Vacuum that does not greatly please me, therefore I am in Haste for it to be replenished with other Observations.

These will very soon amply repair the Losses you have sustained by them, answered I. It would be well if every thing else in the World that does us an Injury, would make as good a Compensation for it.

Imagine yourself to be in a Place of *Milton*'s visible Darkness, or rather still darker a Place, if you will be absolutely deprived of all Light; and this shall be our Theatre of Reasoning and Observations.

Let a Ray of the Sun enter in at a Hole made in the Window-Shutter, and let a Glass Prism be placed horizontally at this Hole, to refract the Ray in such a Manner as to throw it upon a Wall opposite to the Window, so that as it is going out of the Prism, it is almost horizontal and parallel to the Pavement of the Chamber; whereas if it had

had not been refracted, but direct, it would fall upon the Pavement itself, and there form a white Image of the Sun of a Figure almost round. That Spectrum, or Image of the Sun, which the refracted Ray forms upon the Wall, is very different from that which the direct Ray formed upon the Pavement; for as the Image of the direct Ray was almost round and entirely white, that of the refracted Ray is of a Figure nearly resembling a Fish at Cards, and varied with an infinite Number of Colours, among which the seven primary ones are distinguished and placed in a shining Order, one after another.

The jolly Peacock spreads not half so fair
The eyed Feathers of his pompous Train;
Nor golden IRIS *so bends in the Air,*
Her twenty-colour'd Bow through Clouds of Rain,) FAIRFAX.

I am very glad to find that *Tasso*, said the Marchioness, who had before a little transgressed against the Laws of Refraction for the sake of his *Armida*, has amended his Fault, and is at present reconciled to Optics.

Theſe Colours, anſwered I, with which the Image is painted, are diſpoſed in ſuch a Manner, that the red is in its lower Extremity; above this is placed the orange, afterwards the yellow, then the green and blue indigo, and laſtly the violet, which is placed in the upper Part of the Image. Innumerable Degrees of intermediate Colours inſenſibly connect and unite the ſeven primary ones. Neither *Correggio*, *Titian*, nor his Rival *Roſalba* did ever unite and ſhade their Mezzo Tinto's with ſo much Exactneſs to form the Oval of a Face.

In order to explain this great Change, we muſt ſuppoſe one of theſe two Caſes, either that Light is compoſed of Rays differently coloured and differently refrangible, ſo that the Priſm does nothing but ſeparate them from each other when they are tranſmitted through it; and by this means the different Colours are formed, and the Image which would otherwiſe be round, is of an oblong Figure. This is one manner of explaining this Phænomenon. The other is, that the Light in paſſing through

through a Prism, acquires Colours which it had not before, and moreover, that every Ray is shattered, dilated, and split into many other diverging Rays painted of a different Colour; and this is the Reason why the Image is coloured, and of an oblong Figure.

This last is the Supposition of *Grimaldo*, a Philosopher, who preceded Sir *Isaac Newton*; and this System is called the *Dispersion* of Light. You see it is necessary, unless we admit the different Refrangibility, to suppose this Dispersion, in order to explain why the coloured Image of the Sun should have a Length much greater than its Breadth, after being refracted by the Prism.

This Experiment, said the Marchioness, which has cost me so much Attention to understand, and this Oblongitude of the solar Image, are not sufficient to prove the different Refrangibility, because all this Phænomenon may be as well explained by *Grimaldo*'s Dispersion of the Light, which is a System very different from Sir *Isaac Newton*'s. I want to see some Experiment, which cannot poſſibly be explained by any other Syſtem than the *Newtonian*, and that I believe would ſatisfy me. This, anſwered I, is the very thing neceſſary to prove not only the different Refrangibility, but every other Principle in Philoſophy; and this Sir *Iſaac Newton* has done (without knowing, perhaps, that it would one Day give Pleaſure to a fine Lady) whatever a certain Author may ſay to the contrary, who accuſes him with having drawn more Conſequences from his Obſervations than he ought to have done, one of the greateſt Faults that a Mathematician can be charged with. This Author reproaches Sir *Iſaac* with having inferred the different Refrangibility of the ſolar Rays from the preceeding Obſervations; whereas Sir *Iſaac* declares in expreſs Terms, that the Obſervation is not ſufficient for that Purpoſe, becauſe this ſtrange Appearance of the Image may proceed from the Shattering of the Rays, as *Grimaldo* ſuppoſes; or from an Inequality of Refractions, not conſtant, but only caſual, and therefore can have nothing deduced from

from it. The more ſcrupulous this great Philoſopher appears in his Reaſons, the more licentious does his Adverſary ſeem in his Accuſation. In order to remove the Diſperſion of *Grimaldo*, and the fortuitous Inequality of the Refractions, he invented the following Experiment, which is as it were the Arbitrator and Judge of the Controverſy.

He received the coloured Image formed by the Priſm, and caſt upon the Wall, upon the Face of another Priſm placed upright, in ſuch a Manner, that the red of the Image ſhould fall upon the lower, and the violet in the ſuperior Part of this Face, and the other intermediate Colours ſhould fall reſpectively in the intermediate Spaces betwixt the red and the violet.

If the firſt Priſm, which was placed horizontally, refracted the Rays upwards, this ſecond, placed upright, muſt refract them ſideways, either on the right or the left; ſo that if they were at firſt thrown almoſt directly upon the Wall oppoſite to the Window, they muſt now ſtrike it obliquely, and

 with

with ſome Inclination. The Refraction then which the Colours are to ſuffer in paſſing ſideways thro' this ſecond upright Priſm, is the Thing which muſt determine the Queſtion, either in Favour of Sir *Iſaac Newton*'s Suppoſition of the different Refrangibility, or for *Grimaldo*'s Notion of the Shattering of the Rays, or laſtly, muſt give the Preferrence to a fortuitous and caſual Inequality of the Refractions, which cannot agree with any Syſtem at all. For, if the ſolar Image, formed by the firſt Priſm which refracted the Rays upwards, received its Colours and oblong Figure from a Diſperſion or Dilatation of every incident Ray, a ſecond tranſverſe and ſideways Refraction cauſed by the ſecond Priſm, muſt after the ſame manner ſhatter and dilate the Rays of this Image ſideways, and render it of the ſame Oblongitude in Breadth as it had before been in Length; ſo that a new Image would be painted upon the Wall of the Chamber which is behind the ſecond Priſm; and this Image would be coloured differently from what it

was

was before, and be changed from an oblong Figure, to one almoſt ſquare.

Laſtly, if the Colours and oblong Figure of the Image formed by the firſt Priſm, were occaſioned by a fortuitous and accidental Inequality of Refractions, who can tell what Variations Chance might have produced in the Combination of the ſecond Priſm, and in the new Refraction which that Priſm gave to the Light?

But whatever Effect Chance might produce in this Caſe, it is certain it could never agree with what the *Newtonian* Syſtem aims at. According to this Syſtem, if the colouring and oblong Figure of the Image formed by the firſt Priſm, were occaſioned by the Separation of Rays differently coloured ane differently refrangible, a ſecond Refraction made ſideways can only incline this Image, and muſt leave it juſt the ſame as it was before with regard to its Colours and oblong Figure.

How will it *incline* the Image, ſaid the Marchioneſs? I do not underſtand the Reaſon of this. You will ſoon underſtand it, anſwered I, when you reflect, that if the ſecond Priſm was removed, the Rays would all ſtrike the Wall almoſt in a direct Line. Now if the ſecond Priſm refracts the violet Rays, that is, turns them ſideways and tranſverſly out of their Path, more than it does the red, thoſe muſt ſtrike the Wall more obliquely than theſe, or in other Words, the violet muſt fall at a greater Diſtance from the Priſm than the red. The intermediate Colours too, between the red and the violet, will fall upon intermediate Places of the Wall: Thus the Image will appear inclined, and as it were leaning with its violet Extremity farther from the Priſm than the red is. Theſe Effects muſt happen according to Sir *Iſaac Newton*'s Syſtem; and theſe in reality do happen, as I myſelf have often had the Pleaſure of ſeeing.

If after the ſecond Priſm there be placed a third and fourth, in order that the Image may be ſucceſſively refracted ſideways through them all. Thoſe Rays which were refracted more than

than the rest in the first Prism, will be more refracted too in the following Prisms. But the Image will not be dilated sideways, nor coloured differently from what it was at first.

Nature, said the Marchioness, has pronounced the grand Judgment, and of three Systems that contended for it, the *Newtonian* has carried the golden Apple. I must confess this Decision does not displease me; for to say nothing of the accidental Inequality of Refractions which does not deserve the Prize, *Grimaldo*'s Supposition of the Shattering and Dilatation of every particular Ray, had something too perplexed and imbarrassing in it. If you think the Judgment which Nature has pronounc'd in favour of our Philosopher, answer'd I, to be so just, that of his Adversary, whom I lately mentioned, will appear extremely capricious, who asserts, that Sir *Isaac Newton* has, by agreeable Experiments, confirmed the Observations of *Grimaldo*. I am not so greatly surprized at this Adversary, replied the Marchioness, who does not appear to have

have any great Knowledge of the Matter, as at *Grimaldo* himſelf, who neglected to prove the Truth of his Diſperſion of the Rays, by ſo eaſy and ſimple a Experiment as this, which requires nothing more than a ſecond Priſm after the firſt. One would imagine that it ſhould have been very obvious to a Perſon bent upon making a Syſtem. Say rather, anſwered I, to a Perſon long exerciſed in the Arts of Obſervation, for a Love of building Syſtems and making Experiments, are two Things that ſeldom go together. But it generally happens that the moſt ſimple Things are the moſt difficult, and conſequently the longeſt before they are found out. The Circulation of the Blood, for Example, appears to be a very eaſy Diſcovery, and one would imagine ſhould have been very anciently made. When an Orifice is opened in the Arm the Arteries ſwell from the Heart towards the Extremities of the Body, and the Veins, on the contrary, from the Extremities of the Body towards the Heart. This evidently ſhews that certain Veſſels, that is, the Arteries, are

are designed to convey the Blood from the Heart to the extreme Parts, and other Vessels, namely the Veins, to carry it from the Extremities to the Heart. Besides, the Death of *Seneca* might have furnished the Ancients with a physical Experiment as well as a moral Precept. It was impossible that all the Blood should be emitted through the opening of the Veins, unless those of the superior Parts had a Communication with those of the inferior; or in other Words, unless it circulated through the whole Body. It appears then that it was much easier for the Ancients to discover the Circulation of the Blood, who had so many Experiments ready prepared to their Hands, than for *Grimaldo* to find the Falshood of his Dispersion, because his Experiments must have been the Effect of his own Labour and Invention.

It is true, some Bigots for Antiquity pretend to find this Discovery in *Hippocrates*, so that according to them, all the Inventions of the Moderns, and all our Distempers were known to the Ancients.

cients. But this Notion is the ſame as if a *Vellutellus*, or ſome other zealous Admirer of *Petrarch* ſhould diſcover the *Newtonian* Syſtem of Optics in theſe Verſes,

While the great Author of his Frame expires,
The conſcious Sun withdraws his active Fires;
Pale ſickly Shades ov'rſpread his languid Ray,
And ev'ry beauteous Colour fades away.

The moſt ſimple Things are generally diſcovered the lateſt, and with the greateſt Difficulty. This Aphoriſm, ſaid the Marchioneſs, is too well verifyed even in the Toilet, where an elegant, but ſimple Diſpoſition of our Hair or our Patches, often coſts great Trouble, and the utmoſt Anxiety of Mind.

According to this Principle, anſwered I, Sir *Iſaac Newton*'s Experiments muſt have coſt him an infinite deal of Labour. For if the preceding Experiment,

ment, to prove the different Refrangibility of the Rays, is at once ſimple, agreeable, and concluſive, all the others which he invented for the ſame Purpoſe are no leſs perfect, and yet appear ſo very obvious, that every one would imagine he himſelf might have as eaſily found out.

How, ſaid the Marchioneſs, is not this Experiment ſufficient to prove the different Refrangibility without ſeeking for any more? Have I acted wrong in ſuffering myſelf to be too eaſily convinced? No, Madam, anſwered I, a Lady cannot err in this Point. But Sir *Iſaac Newton* himſelf does not deſire you ſhould aſſent to his Syſtem ſo ſoon. This Experiment, without Diſpute, is ſufficient to demonſtrate the different Refrangibility, but not to ſatisfy a Philoſopher reſolved to try Nature a thouſand Ways, and put her to a thouſand Proofs, in order to eſtabliſh his Belief on a ſure Foundation. You ſeem, ſaid the Marchioneſs, to repreſent Nature as a Coquet, and Sir *Iſaac Newton* as a jealous Lover, who never thinks he has

Proof

Proof enough of the Fidelity of his Miſtreſs. This, however, anſwered I, was the only Object of his Love. I am very ſorry that I cannot ſhew you all the Experiments which he invented for this Purpoſe, in order to preſent you with the moſt finiſhed and beautiful Piece that philoſophical Jealouſy ever compoſed. But the Parts I ſhall ſhew you will aſſiſt you to form an Idea of the whole, juſt as the Obeliſks and Amphitheatres diſcover the Grandeur of ancient *Rome*. Let me intreat you, ſaid the Marchioneſs, to make me a compleat *Newtonian*. I plainly ſee that by my Converſion I ſhall acquire the Knowledge of Truth without loſing that Pleaſure which I found in being deceived.

In the dark Chamber which we have prepared for our Experiment, continued I, let a white Thread be extended horizontally againſt the Window, but at ſome little Diſtance from it. Let two Rays of the Sun enter at two Holes made in the Window-Shutter, which refracted by the two Priſms, may paint two

two coloured Images upon the oppoſite Wall. When this is done, we muſt recommend ourſelves to the Genius which preſides over Optics, and then patiently wait till the Half of this Thread be illuminated by the red Rays of one Image, and Half of it by the violet Rays of the other. Let the Wall oppoſite to the Window be covered with a black Cloth, that the Colours which would otherways be reflected by the Wall, may not diſturb the Experiment; for at preſent we want no other Colours but thoſe of the Thread, which muſt be alone diſtinguiſhed. This Thread muſt be obſerved through a Priſm placed before the Eyes in ſuch a Poſition, that all the Objects ſeen through it appear higher than they really are. The Thread too will appear to be tranſported higher by the Refraction; but becauſe the violet Half ſhould ſuffer a greater Refraction than the red, it will be much more tranſpoſed than the red, ſo that the Thread will appear divided into two Parts, the one illuminated with violet, the other with red, and

and the red will appear lower than the violet.

This Experiment, if we ſhould exclude every other, is intirely agreeable in all its Parts to the *Newtonian* Syſtem. If the violet Part of the Thread be illuminated with indigo, the Thread will appear leſs divided than at firſt, the indigo Half approaching nearer to the red than the violet did, which muſt neceſſarily happen, becauſe the Difference of Refrangibility beween the indigo Rays and the red, is leſs than that between the red and the violet.

If from Indigo this Half be illuminated with blue, the other Half ſtill remaining red, the Thread will for the ſame Reaſon as I before mentioned, appear leſs divided than at firſt, and ſtill ſucceſſively leſs if it be illuminated with the other Colours in order, green, yellow, and orange, till at length becoming red like the other Half, the Thread will no longer appear broken nor divided in two as at firſt, but whole and continued, becauſe now the Colours of each

Half

Half have no Difference in their Refrangibility.

A like Experiment may be made with a Paper, the one Half coloured with red, and the other blue; placed afterwards upon a black Cloth, and looked at through a Prifm, it will appear broken and divided into two Parts. A Paper illuminated with four Colours, (which I have myfelf feen demonftrated) that is red, yellow, green and blue, ranged one after another in the order I have named them, appeared through a Prifm divided into four Pieces, like the Steps of a Ladder. The blue is fometimes the higheft of all, and fometimes loweft, as the Pofition of the Prifm requires. This Experiment varied in as many Ways as the fruitful Imagination of *Paul Veronefe* would vary the Subject of a Picture, always fucceeded fo well, as to have greatly confirmed this Syftem, if its Author had fuffered it to need any Confirmation.

I muft ingenuoufly confefs, faid the Marchionefs, that tho' I have always regarded the Mathematicians with a fingular

gular Veneration, I do not yet understand what their Demonſtrations are. However familiar they may at preſent be rendered, I do not comprehend them enough to find the Solution of a Problem among the Patch-Boxes and Perfumes on my Toilette. I now begin to fear that my Ignorance of the Deity I worſhipped greatly increaſed my Veneration for it. Their Evidence cauſes ſo great a Noiſe in the World, that I was perſwaded every thing elſe, however well it might be proved, had only a ſmall Degree of Probability when compared with theſe. At preſent, I cannot conceive it poſſible for any mathematical Demonſtration to be more certain than Sir *Iſaac Newton*'s different Refrangibility, and yet this is a thing merely phyſical. But you are to conſider, Madam, that the Perſon who has treated upon this phyſical Subject, was the greateſt Mathematician that ever appeared in the World. We may affirm then, replied the Marchioneſs, that as every thing which *Midas* touched was transformed to Gold, ſo every thing that

that Sir *Isaac Newton* handled became Demonstration.

If ever Physics could hope to vye in Certainty with Geometry, answered I, they might with some reason expect it when treated by Sir *Isaac Newton*, tho' there is a very great Difference in the Nature of their Proofs.

Physics can only consider a vast Number of Particulars, make Observations upon them, and thence deduce general Propositions, whereas Geometry by a more expeditious and certain Way, abstracts particular Cases, and founds its Demonstrations upon Nature; and the Idea of the Thing itself, whereon it treats.

All that a Mathematician demonstrates to you concerning one Triangle, will be true in all, be they of what Species they will, because he considers nothing but what is necessarily included in the Nature of a Figure terminated by three right Lines; and as this is found in all Triangles that can possibly be either made or imagined, his Proposition will hold true in all.

On

On the other Hand, a Naturaliſt will tell you, that all Bodies here below gravitate, and if left to themſelves deſcend; but he does not, like the Mathematician, deduce this Propoſition from the Nature of Body, (for that is unknown to him) but from a daily Obſervation that Gold, Silver, Gems, Water, Air, and a thouſand other Bodies gravitate, and do it conſtantly by Day and Night, in Summer and Winter, fair and cloudy Weather; from whence it may reaſonably be inferred by Induction, that every other Body gravitates at all Times, and in all Places.

But however reaſonable this Method may ſeem, ſo great a demand for Proofs implys a Want of Demonſtration, juſt as a too great Attention to Dreſs, argues ſome Defect of natural Beauty in a Face. Who can tell, but notwithſtanding ſuch a Multiplicity of Obſervations, ſome may queſtion whether there be not a certain Body with which we are yet unacquainted, that has no Gravitation? Or if there be not ſome Country in the unknown Tracts of the ſouthern Pole, where Bodies have not that Quality of Gravitation which we diſcover them to be indued with in all the known World? Or laſtly, whether in paſt Ages there may not have exiſted a certain Body that did not gravitate? You will grant, however, ſaid the Marchioneſs, that where the Number of Obſervations is ſo great as that from whence the Gravitation of Bodies, and the different Refrangibility of the Rays of Light are deduced, that Perſon muſt be inexcuſable who doubts their Evidence, unleſs it was preſcribed him by a Phyſician for his Health.

If there are ſome, anſwered I, too exceſſive in their Doubts, there are many others too bold in their Aſſertions. All do not imitate the prudent and neceſſary Reſerve of our judicious Philoſopher: Some are contented with one ſingle particular Caſe, from which they haſtily deduce a general Concluſion, like thoſe who form a Judgment of the Temper and general Character of a whole Nation from the particular Humour of a ſingle Perſon, whom they have ſeen perhaps once or twice at a Coffee-Houſe.

Sir

Sir *Isaac Newton's* Antagonist whom I lately mentioned, imagining he had overthrown the System, and principally the different Refrangibility, in order to prove himself the Opponent of this great Author, even in the Method of philosophising, has put together a general System (hinted at by others, but not followed) formed upon particular Cases, which well examined, are nothing but Consequences of that which he imagined himself to have overthrown. He supposes certain Grounds, and a Mixture of Light and Shade; and the different Combinations of these are according to his Opinion, the Cause of different Colours —— Can a Combination of Light and Shade, interrupted the Marchioness, ever produce red or yellow? A Phænomenon must be very unfortunate, whose Explication depends on this System. Perhaps, answered I, those Phænomena which contradict general Laws, those Monsters of Optics, if there are any such, are sent by Nature to this System for their Explication; and do not these fine Colours of of yours to, deserve a little Punishment for all the Mischiefs they have caused? But see the unhappy Condition of the poor prismatic Colours, which certainly do not merit the Correction that yours do; and from hence you may form an Idea of the Value of this System.

It affirms, that when a Ray of the Sun is refracted by a Prism, these Colours are produced by means of two sorts of Images; the one formed by the Dispersion of the solar Rays, and the other by that of the Rays of Heaven, which are contiguous to those of the Sun. What, said the Marchioness, does this Philosopher attempt to bring this *Dispersion* again upon the Stage? Had he never seen the Experiment of the second upright Prism, which has for ever banished this Supposition from the Province of Optics?

Authors, answered I, have their Eyes formed differently from those of other Men. The Sun is light, and the Sky comparatively dark. This was sufficient to furnish the Philosopher we are speaking of, with Abundance of Relations betwixt Light and Shade (the Veils, as he expresses it, formed by these two Images) from whence he draws an Explication of the Difference of Colours in a Prism. I fancy, said the Marchioness, this Explication will not be very simple; it appears to me sufficiently perplexed. Not to insist upon this and many other Difficulties which this System is chargeable with, we will confine ourselves to the following Objection, answered I.

If it be true that this Diversity of Colours depends on a Mixture of the Rays of these two Images of the Sun and Sky, and from their shaddowing each other, it is certain that if there can be found a Method to prevent the celestial Rays from coming to the Prism, and consequently from being refracted and mixt with those of the Sun, the Colours will vanish with all that fine Theory which arises from the Mixture of those two sorts of Rays.

Now this may easily be effected, if before the Ray of the Sun (which enters at the Window of the dark Room) be be refracted by the Prism, the Middle of the Ray be transmitted through another Hole made in a Table, or a Pastboard placed at some Distance from the Window: In this Case so far is the Prism from receiving the celestial Rays contiguous to those of the Sun, that it receives no Rays from the Sun himself, but what flow from his Disk, and is not at all affected by those which proceed from his Edge. It is evident then that if this System be true, the Colours of the Images in this Case could not appear, which is absolutely contrary to Experience, a Disgrace pretty familiar to this System.

You seem, said the Marchioness, to resemble *Bacchus* throwing down the Giants, who attempted to dethrone the Gods, in order to usurp their Places. The Spirit of Ambition appears no less strong in this Author, than in those presumptuous Sons of Earth.

You are to suppose, answered I, that an Author is often as strongly desirous of giving his Name to a new System, as a *French* Lady can be of giving her's to a new Fashion. How happy would they be, if, like that *Chinese* Emperor, who burnt all the Books of History preceding his Reign in order to make his Name the first Epocha of it, they could destroy all preceding Systems to make their own the Epocha of human Knowledge.

Besides, Sir *Isaac Newton*'s System came from a Country too far beyond the *Alps*, to be favourably received among *Italians*. It would be very surprizing, if a System, produced in *England*, had not been treated with Aversion by some Persons in a Country so near the Sun as ours. I do not see, replied the Marchioness, why a System should meet with the worse Usage for being a Native of *England*. For my Part, as much an *Italian* as I am, I do not believe that I should be prejudiced against a well grounded one, even if it had been produced in *Ireland*, or *Nova Zembla*.

You are not to imagine yourself, answered I, to be ranked with the Generality of Mankind. A Sea, a River, or a Chain of Mountains placed between some

ſome People and a certain Truth, are inſuperable Objections to their Reception of it. Perhaps as the *Romans* found a certain *Je ne ſçais quoi*, in the Stile of *Livy*, which diſcovered the *Paduan*, ſo our *Italians* find a *Je ne ſçais quoi*, in every Truth that comes from beyond the *Alps*, which does not agree with their Taſte. Theſe Gentlemen, ſaid the Marchioneſs, muſt have a very diſtinguiſhing Judgment to diſcover ſuch Differences as theſe, or it rather argues, they have no Taſte for Truth, who find any thing foreign in the Proofs of a different Refrangibility. In this I may venture to affirm myſelf a better *Italian* than they, ſince the leaſt Difference in this Caſe muſt turn to our Diſadvantage.

You, Madam, ſaid I, are a Citizen of the World, and your Senſes formed for Truth are Proof againſt the Objections of thoſe who only appear to be zealous for it. You will find a new Demonſtration of the different Refrangibilities drawn from the Difference in the Focus of a Lens, through which the different Colours are viewed.

The Image of the Letters of a Book, formed by a Convex Glaſs, illuminated by the red Rays of a Priſm appears diſtinct at a certain Diſtance from the Glaſs: The Image of the ſame Letters, when illuminated by the blue Rays, is not diſtinct, but at a leſs Diſtance. In the like Manner, the four Colours, red, yellow, green, and blue, of the Paper we before mentioned, are not equally diſtinct when placed at an equal Diſtance from the Lens. The blue is neareſt, next follows the green, afterwards the yellow, and laſt of all the red, whoſe Rays being leſs refrangible than the reſt, muſt be collected and united at a greater Diſtance from the Lens.

Might not ſome wiſe Caviller, ſaid the Marchioneſs ſmiling, gravely object, that the Book which firſt received the red, and afterwards the blue Rays, was wrote in *Engliſh*; and that in order to prove the different Refrangibility, it was neceſſary for it to be *Italian*? But after all, it is an infamous Thing to be ſo hardened againſt Truth. Are not theſe

Expe-

Experiments ſufficiently deciſive? And can there in any Country of the World be aſſigned a Cauſe, why the Image of one Colour ſhould be nearer to a Lens than that of another, unleſs it be the different Refraction which they ſuffer in paſſing through the Lens. Do not put yourſelf in a Paſſion, Madam, ſaid I, the different Refrangibility will be true, notwithſtanding theſe Objections. You may ſtill ſafely believe it, as many other judicious Perſons do, in Defiance of that obſtinate War which the Antagoniſt of our Philoſopher declared againſt it. The *Newtonian* Syſtem had the ſame Fortune as that Field where *Hannibal* encamped when he beſieged *Rome*, which did not ſell at all the worſe upon that Account: Or rather, you may look upon theſe Objections as the ſatyrical Verſes, thoſe miſerable Invectives which the Licentiouſneſs and Malignity of the common Soldiers, mixt with the Acclamations and Glory of a *Roman* Triumph. The Beauty and Simplicity of this Syſtem did not deſerve to paſs unmoleſted by Envy and

Cenſure, that Tax which Merit is bound to pay to the Public.

A celebrated Miniſter (*) at once capable of the ſublimeſt Projects and the loweſt Employments, and a whole College, joined their Forces againſt the Applauſes paid to the *Cid*. For a like Reaſon *Moliere*'s *Miſanthrope* was recited to the ſame Audience that liſtened to the Sermons of *Cotin*. How often have the celebrated *Caracci* had the Mortification of ſeeing their fine Pieces ſold in their Life-time by the *Ell*, (if I may uſe that Expreſſion) which now are the Ornaments of the beſt choſen Galleries, and paid by the Admiration of Connoiſſeurs, better than by the Gold of the Rich!

It was neceſſary for the Honour of Sir *Iſaac Newton*'s Syſtem, that it ſhould be attacked on all Sides, and that ſome ſhould diſpute the different Refrangibility of the Rays, while others wrangle about the *Immutability of Colours*, which is another of their Properties diſcovered by our penetrating Philoſopher.

(*) Cardinal *Richelieu*.

The

The Experiment upon which this new Quality of Colours is principally founded, was renewed in *France* by Monſieur *Mariotte*, a Man exceedingly well verſed in the Arts of Obſervation. This Experiment in his Hands produced an Effect contrary to what Sir *Iſaac Newton* had given Reaſon to hope for. Thus a Syſtem, the ſlow and conſiderate Off-ſpring of Reaſoning and Experience, was eſteemed imaginary and vain; and a grave Philoſopher, who ſpent his whole Life in the Study of Truth, paſſed for a Reveur, or an Impoſtor.

What is this you tell me, ſaid the Marchioneſs, of an Experiment in *France* contrary to that of Sir *Iſaac Newton*? Is it poſſible that two Men equally attentive and accuſtomed to Obſervation, ſhould need a third to decide a Matter of Fact? It is not ſurprizing that two People ſhould reaſon differently upon the Circumſtances of a Fact according to their different Principles, as in the Caſe of a Perſon who ſhifted his Linnen three times a Day, one aſſerted that he muſt be extremely neat, and the other that he was a very Sloven. But to dispute and mutually to deny the Fact itself, I always thought reserved for silly Women and Enthusiasts.

It is certainly, answered I, a great Reflection upon Philosophers, when we find them diffent in Matters like these; it at least demonstrates that one of them must have been inattentive in observing the Laws of Nature. Those rational Horses so far superior to us Men, which *Gulliver* discovered in the Island of the *Houyhuynms*, the last Place where he arrived at in his allegorical Voyages, were extremely surprized to find such Contradictions among our Philosophers, that is, those of our Species who take the most Pains to cultivate their Reason. These happy Animals know not the Meaning of Uncertainty and Doubt in Matters of Fact. The Dishonour that Philosophers receive upon this Account is very great even among us, and there are too many Examples of it.

Two famous Academies which have equally Truth for their End, and Emulation for their Companion and Guide, disputed

disputed upon a Fact, by which is demonstrated the Refraction which Light suffers in passing from a Vacuum into Air. That Academy which maintained the Refraction was at length victorious; and it was necessary that even this Truth should be contested in order to be admitted. Some from Experience will tell you, that in breathing, the Air passes from the Lungs to the Heart, while others alledge the same Experiment to prove that it does not. Many discover certain little Machines and Organizations in the Glands of a Body, which others affirm cannot be seen. Fancy and Prepossession have the same Influence here as in all other Things, and make us think we discover in Objects, without us, what runs strongest in our own Mind. Thus a few irregular Strokes will appear to the Eyes of a Painter the Contour of a Leg or a Face, Wind-mills become Giants to *Don Quixot*, and Fires and Beeches seem transformed to a fine Lady in the Eyes of a Lover.

An Observator must not search into Ex-

Experiments in order to find his own Opinions there, like that Perſon who looked for his Pedigree in *Homer*, becauſe both the one and the other will every where meet their own Imaginations. Natural Philoſophy, like Poetry, requires a Man formed expreſsly for it, a *Malpighi*, a *Reaumur*, a *Boyle*, not moved by Authority, ſeduced by Fancy, nor terrified by Difficulties, a Man, (if we will believe a celebrated Writer) dexterous, active, and curious as the *French* and *Engliſh*, and reſerved, cautious and circumſpect as the *Italians* and *Spaniards*. Why not the Patience of ſome other Nation, ſaid the Marchioneſs, inſtead of the Caution of ours, which is too like Diffidence to redound greatly to our Honour. This Author, anſwered I, conſiders only the good Qualities of different Nations. But you would be better pleaſed, perhaps, if the Part we contribute to the Formation of a perfect Philoſopher, were the religious Attention of our paſſionate Lovers. I am acquainted with one of

theſe,

these, said the Marchioness, who would be a *Newtonian*, if Philosophy was his Mistress.

This Attention, answered I, might carry these Gentlemen to a great Height of Superstition, as it does a Naturalist, who prescribes it as a Rule of Art, whenever an Experiment is made, to mark exactly the Country, Hour of the Day in which it was effected, what Wind blew at that Time, the Degree of Heat, and Drought of the Air, with many other Circumstances of this Nature, which in some Cases may be proper, and even absolutely necessary, but in others I really do not see of what Service they are, for in looking upon a Paper of two Colours with a Prism, it is of no Sort of Importance whether the Wind blows East or West, whether the Time of the Year be Autumn or Spring, the seventh or twentieth Day of the Month. These circumstantial Naturalists resemble an Antiquarian, who should copy the Cornice of an Inscription with as much Exactness as the Inscription itself.

Physic,

Phyſic, replied the Marchioneſs, has almoſt diveſted itſelf of the Prejudice of obſerving certain Seaſons of the Moon, as a proper Time to apply its Medicines; and perhaps Natural Philoſophy has aſſumed it in her Stead, that theſe ſuperſtitious Notions may not be deſtroyed, but there may always be pretty near an equal Doſe of them in the World.

It muſt be confeſſed, however, anſwered I, that there may always be hoped ſome good Effects from this diligent Diſpoſition, even tho' it be carried to ſuch a Degree as to become ridiculous: But we can never expect any Good from Negligence. You will ſee an evident Proof of this, in that celebrated Experiment of Sir *Iſaac Newton*, before which all the ancient Idols of Optics fall to the Ground; thoſe imaginary Syſtems which ſuppoſed Colour might be changed by Refraction, Reflection, the Continity to Shadow; and in ſhort, that Colour is nothing but a certain Modification, as they expreſs it, it, of Light, which may eafily be changed by thefe Circumftances.

But Sir *Isaac Newton* has fhewn the Falfhood of this Opinion, and demonftrattd that a Ray, for Example, red, well feparated from all the reft, will conftantly keep its Colour in Spite of any Refraction or Reflection it is made to fuffer, or any other Method that the fruitful Invention of a Naturalift can contrive to torment it. The fame Conftancy will hold good in all the other Colours, if they are well feparated. The grand Experiment which furnifhes us with thefe agreeable and furprizing Truths, is this which follows.

The Image of the Sun formed by the Conjunction of a Prifm and Lens is received upon a Paper; by this Conjunction the Colours are much more unmixed and better feparated than they would otherways be.

Having thus made a more perfect Separation, the Rays of different Colours muft pafs fucceffively through a Hole in the Paper, that they may be refracted

refracted by a ſecond Priſm, in order to prove whether this new Refraction can produce any new Colour. If it ſhould, we muſt confeſs that Colour is nothing more than a certain Modification which the Light acquires in paſſing through the Priſm; and then Philoſophers may ſet their Imaginations to work, in order to find out what Notions, Figures, and the like, are neceſſary to produce this Modification.

But on the other Hand, if the Ray conſtantly preſerves its own Colour without the leaſt Alteration, we muſt agree that Refraction has no Share in the Production of Colours, and abandon the ancient Syſtem of Modification; and all its ingenious deluſive Dreams will vaniſh at the riſing Morn of the *Newtonian* Truth.

Now the Experiment we are upon, demonſtrates that a homogeneal Ray, red, yellow, blue, or of any other primary Colour, is not in the leaſt altered, by a new Refraction, nor even by a great Number of Refractions which it is ſucceſſively made to ſuffer. It is not changed

changed either in its Colour or Degree of Refrangibility, which remains constantly the ſame. Thus if two Rays, one red, and the other violet, be made to fall one after another upon the ſecond Priſm, with the ſame Incidence (that is, if both the Rays coming from the ſame Point, fall likewiſe upon the ſame Point of the Priſm.) If the Rays, I ſay, fall upon the ſecond Priſm in this manner, the violet after the ſecond Refraction, will ſtrike the oppoſite Wall in a Situation higher than the red, and the intermediate Colours in intermediate Situations, thoſe which had ſuffered the greater Refraction in the firſt Priſm, ſuffering the greater in the ſecond likewiſe; all theſe Colours will paint upon a white Paper directly oppoſite to them, a little Circle perfectly round, and not oblong like the Image made by the firſt Priſm, and this Circle will be of the ſame Colour as the Rays, without any Addition or Mixture.

I beſeech you to ſtop and take Breath, ſaid the Marchioneſs, you were ingaged in ſuch a long Period, that I began to think

think you would never get to the End of it. I ſhould be ſorry, Madam, anſwered I, if the Length of the Period has rendered me obſcure, and made you loſe ſo fine an Experiment. No, no, ſaid the Marchioneſs, I underſtand it very well. Does not all your Meaning amount to this, that the homogeneal Rays of Light are immutable both with Reſpect to Colour and Degree of Refrangibility? I am extremely rejoiced, ſaid I, to find I may be as prolix in my Periods as I pleaſe, without Apprehenſion of Obſcurity, and may employ one as long as thoſe of the *Azolain* Dialoguiſts, to tell you that this is the Experiment which Mr. *Mariotte* endeavoured to make, and by ſome Misfortune found that after the ſecond Refraction certain new Colours were united to the red and blue. I know not how this happened, but probably it was from ſome Defect in the Priſm which he employed.

The ill Succeſs of this Experiment would have done the Immutability of Colour no ſmall Injury in the learned World

World beyond Sea, if it had not been repeated in *England* before ſome learned *Frenchmen*, the Motive of whoſe Voyage was purely philoſophical. This Repetition of the Experiment clearly demonſtrated, that Mr. *Mariotte*, tho' otherways an accurate Obſerver, has failed in ſome of the Circumſtances neceſſary to bring it to good Effect. Thus were theſe two Nations more divided by their different Ways of thinking, than by a little Arm of the Sea, reconciled upon this Point.

This Law of Nature common to all Nations acquainted with Light, met with a leſs favourable Reception in *Italy* than in any other. The moſt obſtinate Antagoniſts of the *Newtonian* Syſtem have riſen among us; there ſeems to be ſome Fatality in this, that a Nation which the *Italians* once found ſo difficult to ſubdue by Force, ſhould in its Turn find us the moſt difficult to be ſubdued by Reaſon.

In order to contribute my Share to the Eſtabliſhment of this Law even among us, I cauſed the ſame Experiment

ment to be repeated at a Place in *Italy*, celebrated for the learned Men it has always produced, and neuter enough not to be ſuſpected of Partiality. No Miniſter of State, ſaid the Marchioneſs, could act more politickly in the Choice of a proper Place for the holding a Congreſs. Within a very little, anſwered I, all my Politics would have ſignified nothing: For tho' we made uſe of Sir *Iſaac Newton*'s own Method in ſeparating the Colours, and the Chamber was extremely dark, yet a certain Light of a blueiſh Caſt always mixt itſelf with the Colours refracted by the ſecond Priſm. 'Tis true, this Light was irregular and inconſtant, but however, it was ſufficient to ſerve for an Excuſe to the Incredulous.

This Appearance gave us a real Inquietude; and we would never have ſlept in Peace if we had not, after much Study, found out the Cauſe. We obſerved that the Borders of the coloured Image were not ſo well terminated as they ought to have been, provided the Priſm, by which it was coloured, had been

been good. We discovered a Light round the Edges of the same Nature with that which was observed to be mixed with the Colours refracted the second time, and we perceived that several Streaks of this Light crossed the Image from one End to the other. From all these Circumstances it appeared, there must be several Irregularities in the Prism, as Bubbles of Air inclosed in the Glass, Unevenness in the Surface, and other Things of the like Nature, which were probably the Reason why the Light was irregularly refracted, and by this means rendered it impossible for the Colours upon the Image to be perfectly separated.

Various and repeated Experiments made it evident that the Fault of this apparent Alteration of Colours, which we observed in the Image, must be imputed intirely to that irregular Light which we had before suspected to be the Cause, if we may call that an Alteration which was nothing but the Addition of one Colour to another.

I congratulate you, interrupted the Marchioneſs, that after ſuch a Diſcovery nothing will hereafter diſturb the Tranquility of your Sleep. Heaven preſerve me, anſwered I, from that cold tedious Tranquility, which is however the Object of our Deſires. 'Tis in Philoſophy as in all other human Affairs, where the Accompliſhment of one Deſire often gives Birth to another.

When we had diſcovered the Cauſe of this Defect in our Experiments, our next Buſineſs was to find ſome Remedy for it. The Difficulty of acquiring it was a new Motive for our Labour and Inquietude.

Our Priſms in *Italy* are of no other Uſe than to amuſe Children, or hang up as a fine Show in ſome Window in the Country, and not for the Service of Philoſophers, who are often too exact for Artificers, and require a greater Accuracy than is in the Power of Art to beſtow.

We reſolved to write to *England*, which has its *Fawkeners* for Lapidaries, and its *Grahams* for Clock-making, where,

where, in short, every Thing seems to be contrived for the Service of the most curious and importunate Naturalists, if Fortune and our good Genius had not unexpectedly furnished us with some which were just arrived from that Country. These we esteemed as sacred as the *Romans* did the Article or Shield which fell from Heaven in the Reign of *Numa*; and we could have wished for a *Mamurius* to make as many Copies of these as he had formerly done of that.

With one of these Prisms we renewed the Experiment, and the coloured Image painted by it, emerged so beautiful, so well terminated, and so lively, that the other seemed no more, when compared to this, than a rough Draught to a finished Picture. The Colours refracted by a second Prism remained so immutable, that neither the most penetrating Eye, nor even the *Zoilus* of the *Newtonian* System would have discovered the least Alteration.

Perhaps, said the Marchioness, Nature has reserved the Merit of demonstrating Truth to the *English* Prisms, that

that is, to those by whose Means she at first discovered herself. It would be a very curious Phænomenon, answered I, to observe such a Partiality in Nature, as for her to prefer such a Prism made in *London*, to one produced in *Murano*. But the Truth is, that if we consult her as we ought, she always answers the same, whether the Prism be *English* or *Italian*, provided it be good and well worked; and the Chamber, where the Experiment is made, extremely dark.

If all these Circumstances are rightly prepared, the Colours, tho' refracted three or four times, will remain unchangeable, neither more nor less with Regard either to Colour or Figure, than an Object exposed to a homogeneal Light, and viewed through a Prism. The Variety of Colours, the Change of Figure, and the Confusion discovered in Objects looked upon in this Manner, proceeds from nothing but their reflecting more or less all Sorts of Rays, which being afterwards differently refracted, produce all these Irregularities.

If

If upon a Circle of Paper there fall at the ſame time the red of one Image and the blue of another, ſo that the purple Colour, compoſed of both theſe, may appear, it will, when examined through a Priſm, ſeem divided into two ſeparate Circles, the one red and the other blue; and the Reaſon of this Appearance is the different Refraction of theſe two Colours. If the yellow and green of two other Images ſhould fall at the ſame Time upon the Paper, ſo that it would be illuminated with four Colours at once, it will appear oblong and divided by Refraction into as many Circles as there are Colours, and theſe Circles will ſeem placed upon one another. I know you are going to add, ſaid the Marchioneſs, interrupting me, that if this Paper be expoſed to the Light of the Sun, who contains every Sort of Ray in himſelf, it will appear of a Figure ſtill more oblong, and painted with all the Colours of the Rainbow; whereas, if it be illuminated by only one homogeneal Light, it will alter neither its Figure nor Colour when obſerved through a Priſm.

You muſt forgive the Weakneſs of human Nature, Madam, anſwered I, if we generally finiſh the Sentence we have begun. It was reſerved for Sir *Iſaac Newton* and you, to underſtand Nature by half a Word, and find out Natural Philoſophy, notwithſtanding its Uncertainty. It is ſuperfluous to tell you that Flies and other little Objects, placed in a homogeneal Light, appear very diſtinctly to the Eye with a Priſm; and the very ſmalleſt Elziver Print may be read without any Difficulty, But the ſame Things will not have this Effect when placed in the heterogeneous Light of the Sun, becauſe of the Confuſion and Quantities of Colours that ariſe.

In this Caſe I abandon the Priſm to the Diſpoſal of Poetry, to make Uſe of it in Compariſons, which do it no great Honour. That celebrated Author, whoſe fine Ode you ſo much admired, compares it to falſe Eloquence which obſcures the Face of Truth, laviſhes its Orna-

Ornaments without Diſtinction, and diffuſes its glaring Colour over every Thing. It is certain that the Poet in this Compariſon, means that Priſm which tranſmits the Rays of every Sort. And when it tranſmits only the homogeneal Rays, ſaid the Marchioneſs, may we not compare it to true Eloquence and true Spirit? For as it ſhews us the Objects removed out of their Place without any Alteration, ſo true Wit often ſurprizes us only by varying common Subjects in a new Manner.

You are ſo well acquainted with the Priſm, anſwered I, that you may ſafely compare it with your own Wit. But I know not what Compariſon you will find for the Immutability of Colours, unleſs you ſeek for it perhaps in your own Heart; and then knowing that Reflection has no more Influence on that Immutability than Refraction has, you will be better acquainted with it than you at preſent are.

If the Colours with which Bodies are variegated and painted were only a Modification, which the Rays of Light acquire by being reflected from their various Surfaces, as was once believed, a Body which appears red in the Light of the Sun, would ſtill remain red when placed in any other Colour of the painted Image, for Inſtance, *blue*, becauſe it could modify this blue Colour refracted and modified already by the Priſm, as well as it does the Light which comes directly from the Sun.

But Sir *Iſaac Newton* has proved by Experiments, that every Body placed in homogeneal Rays is of the ſame Colour as the Rays themſelves, without allowing, however, the Suppoſition that Bodies by Reflection modify the Light in ſuch a Manner, as to make it receive this or that particular Colour. Thus all white, red, yellow, blue, green Bodies, as Paper, Scarlet, Gold, *Ultramarine*, and Graſs, in red Rays appear totally green, in blue, totally blue, and ſo of the reſt. The only Difference conſiſts in this, that all theſe various Bodies placed in the ſame homogeneal Light, are not all equally luminous, but every Body appears the moſt lively when placed

placed in a Light of its own Colour, except Paper, and all other white Bodies which equally receive any Colour, and may be regarded as the *Cameleon* and *Proteus* of Optics.

Would this Diamond then, interrupted the Marchioneſs, if placed in the Rays of our coloured Image, take indifferently any Colour, and at one Time be transformed to a Ruby, at another to a Topaz, an Emerald or a Saphire? So much the better, anſwered I, as it would dart only one unmixed Colour, and all the varying Slendors with which it ſparkles in the direct Light of the Sun, would vaniſh in this homogeneal Light.

It is very pleaſant to obſerve how the fine Duſt or Atoms in the Air change Colour as they paſs from one Ray to another, juſt as a River varies its Colour according to the various Qualities of its Bottom.

Other Bodies, as I before mentioned, are not equally lively when placed in different coloured Lights. The Varniſh, for Inſtance, with which *Martino*, the Emulator of the *Chinese* Art, makes so many fine Curiosities, is extremely luminous in the red Light, less in the green, and still fainter in the blue. On the contrary, the *Lapis Lazzuli*, which has the Honour to serve for a Repository to your Snuff, is extremely lively in the blue, less so in the green, still fainter in the yellow, and almost dark in the red.

The same Inequality holds good in Bodies seen by a transmitted Light, as is proved by Glasses of different Colours; so that every Body reflects or transmits in great Abundance, those Rays which are of its own Colour, and reflects or transmits the other Rays, in Proportion as they are nearer or farther off its own Colour in the Order of Refrangibility.

It follows from hence, said the Marchioness, that no Colour even that seems the most perfect, can be absolutely unmixed. And perhaps it will never be in the Power of Art to dye a Silk in such a Manner, as for it to reflect only one Sort of Rays.

It would be more difficult, answered I, to sort the various Colours together,

and

and flatter our Sight by the Concords of Harmony, if they were all homogeneal and unmixt. In this Caſe, all the Delicacy of Nature would be requiſite to find out the innumerable intermediate Shades betwixt any two Colours. But now as every Colour is more or leſs blended with ſome other, we are by that Means furniſhed with a much more eaſy and expeditious Way.

Hence it is that the Gradation from one Shade to another (tho' perhaps there may be ſeveral intermediate ones wanting) does not appear defective to our Eye, which diſcovers in each the ſame Baſis of all the Colours that ſoftens them, and ſerves for a Support to the Harmony.

There would ariſe other Inconveniencies beſides theſe, if coloured Mediums did not tranſmit every Sort of Ray; for this would aggravate a Diſtemper bad enough in itſelf, which infects and tinges the whole Body, and the Eye itſelf with an unpleaſing yellow.

Perſons under ſuch Circumſtances as

these, when it is very improper to pay Visits to Ladies, would become absolutely blind, unless to yellow Objects, and could see no Faces but of those who are troubled with the same Disorder.

A perfectly complaisant Lover, replied the Marchioness, if his Mistress should happen to be ill of this Distemper, must cloath himself in yellow, (a Colour which tho' regarded with great Veneration in *China*, is not looked upon as a good Omen for Lovers among us,) and perhaps get the Jaundice in order to be seen by his Charmer, and give her a Proof of his Affection.

So perfect a Lover, answered I, would not be an improper Person to prove this Immutability of Colours, if we had no more Proofs to demonstrate it than what you have already seen. What remained to be shewn was, whether the Confines of Shadow, with which the Light is bounded, are capable of making any Alteration in the Colours? This would have been fine Sport for those Natu-

Naturalists who lay hold on every thing, in order to build a System.

Our Philosopher put the Colours to the Test of this new Experiment, and found nothing wanting in their Constancy which maintains its Ground, even when it happens that Rays of different Colours cross and intersect each other; it appears, in short, to defy every thing judged capable of bringing any Alteration upon them.

We must have Recourse to Romance, said the Marchioness, to find some equal to these Colours, which do not give Place even to the *Ephesian Anthia*, a Model of the firmest and most obstinate Constancy, in Spite of all that a Romancer can produce to make her at length —— What? answered I, resemble the Matron her Fellow-Citizen, reply'd the Marchioness. The Constancy of these Colours must certainly appear very surprizing to Ladies, answered I. I do not doubt but the greater Part of them would much sooner admit the System of *Lucretius*, who, without so many

Experiments, affirmed not only that they are mutable, but that any one Colour may be changed into all the reſt.

The FIFTH DIALOGUE.

THE next Morning, as ſoon as the Marchioneſs was up, ſhe ſent for me into her Cloſet, not concealing that agreeable Diſorder which ſhe knew her Beauty could receive no Injury from. I find indeed, ſaid ſhe, that your Philoſophy begins to grow a very ſerious Thing. I can aſſure you, I have ſlept much leſs this Night than before. I cannot tell whether this be the Reaſon of it, but I find that Philoſophy and ſound Sleep do not agree very well together. My interrupted Dreams have tranſported me into the Region of Optics, where I ſaw nothing but Priſms, Lenſes, Rays differently refracted, coloured Images, in ſhort, all thoſe Experiments, and all that philoſophical Apparatus which you deſcribed, aroſe ſucceſſively in my Imagination

like

like Viſions and Fantomes. Whatever Charms theſe Things may have in themſelves, I could never have imagined they would employ my Thoughts ſo ſtrongly at a Time when it is not very cuſtomary to think of Philoſophy. No really, anſwered I, it was a Time more proper to think on the Philoſopher. You are not to ſuppoſe, replied the Marchioneſs, but he had his Share, and has no Reaſon to complain of me. If this be the Caſe, Madam, anſwered I, there is no great Miſchief done. I rather adviſe you to recal theſe Dreams to your Memory as often as you can, and you will be ſtill the more ſenſible that they deſerve it. How do you ſuppoſe it poſſible, continued ſhe ſmiling, that I could think on theſe Experiments, without admiring the Penetration and Ingenuity of the Philoſopher who invented them, a Man who ſeemed directed by Nature herſelf, in the Method of tracing her Laws? I perceive, ſaid I, that you take the Thing too ſeriouſly. In the preſent Caſe I think you might be contented with the Expoſitor.

How

How can I be too ſerious? replied the Marchioneſs. We are examining whether Colours be immutable or not, whether the Rays of Light be differently refrangible, we are building up and throwing down Syſtems, and in ſhort, our Inquiries aim at nothing leſs than Truth itſelf. Can you reaſonably accuſe me then of being too ſerious in Matters of ſuch Importance? But theſe Syſtems, anſwered I, and this Truth, however pompous they may ſound to the Ear, ought not, however, to diſturb our more agreeable Dreams. It would really gain me a fine Reputation in the World, if it were publickly known that I had made you dream of Lenſes and Priſms. We ſhould act in Things of this Nature, as thoſe who ſtudy to make the beſt Uſe of their Paſſions, do with Regard to Love. Theſe Perſons (who do not appear to be the moſt injudicious) never devote themſelves ſo intirely to it, as to interrupt their more important Concerns, but only as much as is ſufficient to make them paſs away two or three Hours agreeably

agreeably with that Sex with whom it is hardly poſſible to converſe upon good Terms, without at leaſt a Pretence of being in Love.

You at once give me Leſſons in Love and Philoſophy, replied the Marchioneſs. But you know when People firſt fall in Love, they have little Leiſure for theſe grave Reflections, but ſuffer themſelves to be tranſported farther than they ought. This is exactly my Caſe with regard to Philoſophy, in which I have hardly yet advanced one Step. I am ſo little Miſtreſs of myſelf, that I have gone ſo far as to ſeek Methods to confirm Sir *Iſaac Newton*'s Syſtem. After all you have told me, judge whether my Tranſports were not very ſtrong.

Let us ſee, Madam, anſwered I, what they have produced, for we often owe the fineſt Things to ſtrong Paſſions. The *Iliad*, *Æneis*, the Poems of *Dante* and *Milton* were produced in their moſt vigorous Time of Life. To theſe may be added (at leaſt for that Veneration with which they are regarded by their Coun-

Countrymen) the *Luſiade* of *Camoens*, compoſed in a Time of the greateſt Revolutions and Conqueſts in *Portugal*, and the *Araucana* of the *Spaniards*, where the Poet himſelf is the Hero. Perhaps between the broken Slumbers of laſt Night, your Imagination produced ſomething greater than all I have been mentioning.

I am afraid, anſwered the Marchioneſs, that it will amount to very little. I was thinking, that if Light is compoſed of Rays of different Colours, which blended together, produce *white*, we ought to examine whether theſe Colours, after being ſeparated by the Priſm, might not be mixt together again. I for a long Time conſidered, but with little Succeſs, in what Manner this could be effected.

Sir *Iſaac Newton* himſelf, ſaid I, has delivered you from this Trouble; for that Method of confirming his Syſtem which you mention is ſo good, or rather ſo evident and immediate a Conſequence of Order, that he has made ſeveral Experiments to that Purpoſe.

I am now going to ſhew you one of the moſt celebrated, and at the ſame Time the moſt ſimple, to which this great Philoſopher was conducted by that Spirit of Order which you poſſeſs in common with him.

The Image of the Sun made by a Priſm in the dark Chamber, is received upon a Convex Lens, that the coloured Ray, which at going out of the Priſm, diverged, may by the Lens be made to converge and unite, and by this Means be again blended together. I am quite aſhamed both of my Stupidity and myſelf, interrupted the Marchioneſs. I had all the Materials neceſſary for the Execution of my Idea, ready prepared to my Hand; they only wanted putting together, and I had not the Senſe to do it. You were greatly in the Right to be unwilling that a Perſon ſhould hear the Voice of Philoſophy, who is incapable of making it an Anſwer. I might rather, anſwered I, apply to you that famous Saying of Antiquity, *I wiſh with all theſe Qualifications, you were one of us.* You will find in Optics themſelves,

ſelves, ſome Conſolation for what you call your *Stupidity*. Men, thoſe reaſonable and curious Beings, lived above three hundred Years before they found out that a Convex and Concave-Glaſs put together, would make a Telleſcope; and tho' they had the Materials every Day at Hand, were at laſt indebted to mere Chance for this uſeful Inſtrument. It was a greater Diſgrace to Mankind not to diſcover it before, than Honour to them that they found it at laſt. So that this uſeful and fine Invention is of the Number of thoſe which are ſtanding Monuments of the Weakneſs of human Nature. You comfort me, replied the Marchioneſs, at the Expence of Mankind. —— But to return to our Subject. I ſuppoſe that Point beyond the Lens, where the coloured Rays are united, will appear totally white.

The Rays, anſwered I, have no ſooner paſſed through the Lens, but they begin to mix and efface each other; and they loſe the fine harmonious Proportion eſtabliſhed betwixt them in the Spaces of the coloured Image, the Original of the

the Music of the Eyes. When they are all confined at length, and incorporated together in the Focus of the Lens, they form a little circular Image totally white, a Republic (if I may use the Expression) of Colours, where they are all equally tempered together: The red can no longer display its lively Flame, the green boasts no more the smiling Livery of the Spring, nor the blue the lucid Robe of Heaven, but all blended together, restore the Whiteness of the Sun from whence they came, in such a Manner, however, that as they recede from the Focus, they again renew their Splendor and Colour, but in a contrary Order, and the ravished Eye again wanders from one Pleasure to another.

You will easily understand how they come to be inverted, if you remember the two Sticks crossed together, mentioned by *Des Cartes*, which you once believed to have a greater Efficacy in explaining the Phænomena of Optics than they really have. The Appearance that the Colours again make beyond

yond the Place where they were blended, demonſtrates that the Rays loſe neither their Colour nor Quality, as ſome might perhaps believe, but that the Whiteneſs which appears in the Focus of the Lens, is produced only by their Mixture.

I now underſtand, ſaid ſhe, what you meant Yeſterday by ſaying, that the Immutability of Colours ſtill remains, even when Rays of a different Colour interſect and croſs each other; for if it were otherways, we ſhould not ſee the priſmatic Colours re-appear beyond the Place where the Rays united.

This is the very Experiment, anſwered I, upon which the Immutability of Colours was grounded; and all the Experiments of Sir *Iſaac Newton* have this peculiar and admirable Quality, that each ſingle one is not contented with demonſtrating only one Thing, as is the Caſe of moſt others, but demonſtrates many more at the ſame Time. This ariſes from the cloſe Union, and almoſt Geometrical Connexion

nexion which the Properties of Light have between themſelves.

Sir *Iſaac Newton*'s Experiment, ſaid the Marchioneſs, ſeems to reſemble the Battles of the Ancients, which often gained the Victor a great Number of Provinces at a Time. And thoſe of moſt other Philoſophers, anſwered I, the Battles of the Moderns, the moſt noiſy Preparations, the moſt conſummate Contrivance, and the Blood of Millions, amount to no more than the taking a Place, which perhaps might have ſurrendered in two Months by a Treaty.

But to return to your Experiment. I call it *your's*, becauſe tho' you did not invent it, you ſaw the Neceſſity there was for its Invention in order to compleat the Syſtem. Our Philoſopher never quitted it till he had varied it a thouſand Ways.

It was neceſſary to prevent ſome one of the coloured Rays from paſſing through the Lens, in order to ſee whether the Whiteneſs of the little circular Image would by that means be changed.

This

This Sir *Isaac Newton* did, and intercepted the Paſſage ſometimes of one Colour and ſometimes of another; and the Whiteneſs ceaſed, and degenerated into that Colour which ariſes from the Compoſition of thoſe Colours which were not intercepted, but ſuffered to paſs through the Lens.

The Want of any Colour in the circular Image, which is not ſuffered to paſs, will be very agreeably diſcovered by looking thro' a Priſm, which reſolves the Image into its component Colours, by giving them a different Refraction.

If all the Rays be tranſmitted thro' the Lens, the Image will be white; but viewed through a Priſm, it will appear of all Colours like the Rainbow: If any Ray be intercepted, this by the Priſm was diſcover'd to be wanting in the Image, till at laſt ſuffering only one Colour to paſs thro' the Lens, this one Colour too was ſeen by the Priſm.

If all the Colours were ſucceſſively intercepted by the Teeth of a Comb made to paſs very ſwiftly over the Lens, the circular Image would remain white, and

and the different Colours not be diſtinguiſhed, by Reaſon of the quick Impreſſion which they all ſucceſſively make upon the Eye.

You may perhaps have obſerved, that when a lighted Torch is moved nimbly round in a Circle, the whole Circle which it forms in the Air, appears on Fire; and the Reaſon of this is, becauſe the Senſation (which in the ſeveral Places of that Circle it raiſes in the Eye) remains impreſſed till the Torch returns again to the ſame Place.

In the ſame Manner (when the Colours follow one another with an extreme Rapidity) the Impreſſion of each of them remains in the Eye, till a Revolution of all the Colours be compleated. The Impreſſions therefore of all the ſucceſſive Colours are at once in the ſame Part of the Eye, and jointly excite the Senſation of Whiteneſs there.

The ſame was afterwards proved by a Wheel, whoſe Circle, painted with the ſeveral Colours of the Priſm, appeared white, when turned very rapidly round itſelf.

I must confess, said the Marchioness, that even if I could have found the Experiment I sought for, I should never have been able to diversify it so many different Ways, tho' the Inconstancy which you, Gentlemen, lay to our Charge, might perhaps have given me no small Assistance.

This Inconstancy, answered I, which perhaps is not so great a Defect as some believe, was not wanting in Sir *Isaac Newton*. With the most fertile, and almost poetical Imagination, he continually invented new Experiments, which tho' different from each other, all concurred to prove the same Thing. They seemed to rise under his Hands as the Poets make Flowers spring under the Feet of their Beauties.

The coloured Image formed by the Prism becomes white, when viewed thro' another Prism, in such a Manner, that it contracts the Image and mingles the Colours. I have observed the same Phænomenon in the Rainbow, which is the Effect of a Separation of the solar Rays in the Drops of Rain opposite

opposite to the Sun. It appears white when viewed thro' a Prism, turned in such a Manner, as to contract it and blend the Colours together.

Those who live near the Cataracts of Rivers, see a Rainbow every Day, when the Sky is clear, formed by the Sun in the dashing of the Water against the Rocks; making People have the Opportunity of seeing this Experiment much oftner than we can.

I would, if possible, replied the Marchioness, have nothing to envy others. Tho' we have no Cataracts, a Fountain will imitate the Rain, present us with the Colours of the Rainbow, and we may make our Observations at Pleasure. We will call this Fountain, if you think proper, *The Fountain of Optics.*

Till your Garden furnishes you with Proofs of the *Newtonian* System, answered I, as the Gallery did with Objections against the *Cartesian*, you may return to the dark Room: There you will see that the Whiteness of a Paper placed over against the coloured Image of of the Sun, does not ſuffer any Alteration, if it be placed in ſuch a Manner as to partake equally of all the Colours: Whereas, if it approaches nearer to one than another, its Whiteneſs will be tinged with that Colour which is next it. Is it poſſible now for Truth to deſcend from Heaven with a more ſhining Train of Proofs?

I was very confident, ſaid the Marchioneſs, to venture my Thoughts upon a Thing which coſt Sir *Iſaac Newton* ſo much Study. How is it poſſible I could ever have found out the very leaſt of theſe Experiments as eaſy and ſimple as they now appear? But in Exchange, anſwered I, you can eaſily invent Things that perhaps would have puzzled the Philoſopher. It is much more proper for you to know in what Proportion to mix Hope and Fear, Smiles and Frowns, to prevent a Lover's Paſſion from growing languid, than to be exactly acquainted what Quantity of different coloured Powders is neceſſary to be mixed together to form a white. This is another Experiment which our Philoſopher tried, that there might be nothing wanting to confirm his Syſtem. It is true, the white which ariſes from this Compoſition is duſky, grey, and obſcure, like the Colour of Aſhes: And the Reaſon is, becauſe the Colours of theſe Powders are too imperfect and faint, compared with thoſe of the Priſm, to make a lively clear white.

However, if this Mixture be expoſed to the Sun, in order to increaſe the Force of the Light, that duſky obſcure white will become bright and clear, tho' it will never equal the Strength of the Paper expoſed to the ſame Light.

For this Reaſon in coloured Prints, one of the fineſt Inventions of our Time, which, with only three Colours, perfectly imitate all the Variety of Painting, the Paper is left uncovered for *ſtrong Clears* and *Whites.*

Water thickened with Soap, and agitated ſo as to raiſe a Froth, is more proper to demonſtrate that a Compoſition of Colours produces white. After the Froth is a little ſettled, there will appear upon the Surfaces of the Bubbles

of

of which it is compoſed, different Colours, which when viewed at a Diſtance cannot be diſtinguiſhed from each other, and the whole Froth will appear perfectly white. This Experiment has, beſides its being an agreeable one, this further Advantage, that it is very eaſy to make.

Philoſophy, ſaid the Marchioneſs, from what I can diſcover of it, is like a Game of Cheſs, which upon any other Occaſion I ſhould make no Scruple to call an ingenious Pretext to waſte Time. The very leaſt Piece in the one, and the leaſt Experiment in the other, is often of the higheſt Importance. A Pawn in the Hand of a ſkilful Player may give Check Mate, and a little Froth will furniſh Sir *Iſaac Newton* with a whole Magazine of Obſervations and Diſcoveries. Half the World that preceded him had the ſame Bubbles and Froth before their Eyes, without ſo much as ſeeing them. The Ancients themſelves would a thouſand times have obſerved and neglected them.

The Eyes of the Ancients, anſwered

I, were much better able to judge of the Elegance of a Statue or a Temple, than the Importance of an Experiment. *Seneca* was acquainted with a Sort of Priſm, which receiving the Light of the Sun on one Side, diſplayed to the Eye the Colours of the Rainbow. All the Explication which he gives of this Phænomenon is, that there is really no Colour, but only the Appearance of a falſe Colour like that on the Neck of a Dove, which appears and diſ-appears according to the Motion of the Eye and the Change of its Situation. This fine Explication ſufficiently ſhews how very little the Ancients ſtudied Nature and purſued her Steps; for if *Seneca* had taken the leaſt Trouble to examine his Priſm, he muſt have ſeen the Difference between the Colours produced by that, and thoſe on the Neck of a Dove.

A particular Sort of Microſcope known to this Philoſopher, and which perhaps the ancient Artificers made Uſe of in the curious ingraving of their Intaglia's and Cameo's, the Enigma and Admiration of our Time, this Microcroſcope I ſay, compoſed of a Ball of Glaſs filled with Water, had no better Fortune in his Hands than the Priſm. He aſcribed the magnifying of the Objects viewed thro' this Glaſs to a Quality of the Water, and not to the Figure of the Glaſs which contained it.

The Weight and other Properties of Air were known to the Ancients; and in order to explain how Water aſcends in a lifting Pump (which is occaſioned by this Weight of the Air) they had Recourſe to a certain imaginary Horror that Nature has for a Vacuum: So that rather than leave the ſmalleſt Space empty, ſhe choſe to violate her own Laws of Gravity, and make the Water aſcend. And as one Folly produces a thouſand more, the great Horror that Nature teſtified for a Vacuum in this Pump, extended only to a certain Height, and beyond this perhaps was changed into Love, for there ſhe admits as great a Vacuum in the Pump as you could deſire.

But to quote ſtill more Examples ---

Nero in his golden Palace (one of the moſt magnificent Effects of deſpotic Power in the Univerſe) erected a Temple of Stone ſo very tranſparent, that Day-Light entered into it even when the Doors were ſhut. *Pliny* who gives us this Relation, inſtead of contenting himſelf with affirming that it was more tranſparent than Alabaſter, ſays, that it did not tranſmit the Light like other pellucid Subſtances, but included it within itſelf: If this had been the Caſe, the Temple muſt have appeared much more luminous by Night than Day.

The Ancients were fonder of what raiſed their Admiration than increaſed their Knowledge; and perhaps thought Experiments (which are the only Method by which we can arrive to a true Admiration of Nature) were too material to imploy the Attention of a Philoſopher, who ought to conſult nothing but Reaſon. They never imagined theſe Experiments would one Day lead induſtrious Poſterity to ſuch an Exactneſs as to ſubject Flame to the Examination

nation of a Balance, which was antiently regarded as a light Subſtance, for whoſe Sake they invented a particular Sphere of Fire where it was affirmed to aſcend.

Nor could they forſee that theſe Experiments could help us to calculate how much we daily loſe by a continual inſenſible Perſpiration, how many million Tons of Water the Mediterranean Sea perſpires in a Summer's Day, how much a Man decreaſes by the Weakneſs of the Muſcles from Morning to Night? In ſhort, that they ſhould inable us to counterfeit Nature herſelf; and by certain chemical Mixtures emulate her *Etna*'s and *Veſuvio*'s, and imitate her Thunder much better than their own raſh *Salmoneus*.

If an Antient had been aſked whether the Phoſphorus of *Bologna*, for Example, ſhines by its own Light, or by a borrowed one, it is impoſſible to know how many ridiculous Fancies they would have uttered by conſulting Reaſon; whereas a Modern with a ſingle Experiment has put the Matter out of all

Queſtion. Pray what is this *Phoſphorus*, said the Marchioneſs, this Subject of the Abſurdities of the Ancients and Experiment of the Moderns? It is a certain Stone, anſwered I, found in a Mountain near *Bologna*, which calcin'd with Fire, acquires the Property of ſhining in the dark like a Coal, if it has been expoſed a little while to the Light of the Sun, or only to the open Air. From this Quality it has obtained the fine *Greek* Name of *Phoſphorus*, which ſignifies a lucid Body. This is an Honour given almoſt to every Thing appropriated to learned Uſes. An Etymologiſt could not perhaps give a better Name to this Place than that of *Phoſlophus* (which in our Language ſignifies the *Lucid Hill*) and would thus conſecrate it for ever to Philoſophy and Learning. We are much obliged to your Scholar, ſaid ſhe, for conferring ſo fine a Name on this Place which certainly deſerves it.

The Queſtion, continued I, is at preſent reduced to this, whether the *Phoſphorus* only takes in and imbibes the Light

Light to which it is expoſed, and from thence carried into the dark, ſhines with a borrowed Light, or whether the external Light puts its Parts into ſuch an Agitation as to kindle a Light which it contains within itſelf, which by this means looſed from its Priſon, if I may uſe that Expreſſion, emits itſelf from the Phoſphorus, which in this Manner ſhines by its own Light. This laſt Suppoſition is more honourable for it, and better agrees with the fine Name it bears.

In order to decide this Point, a modern Philoſopher choſe a Sort of Light which would ſhew whether the Phoſphorus, when expoſed to it, imbibed any of its Rays, and by that means reveal the Theft of this new *Prometheus.* I already ſee, interrupted the Marchioneſs, how this Modern proceeded. He placed the Phoſphorus in one of the Colours of the priſmatic Image, in order to ſee whether it would acquire the Colour as well as the Light: If it did actually take the Colour, it is evident that it imbibes the external Light, and ſhines with a Splendor not its own:

But if it does not take the Colour of the Image (ſince Colours are immutable and ſuffer no Alteration) the Light only agitates its Parts, and as you expreſs it, loſes its Splendor out of Priſon; and thus the Phoſphorus ſhines not by a borrowed Luſtre but its own, and ought rather to be compared with the Sun himſelf, than *Prometheus*.

It is too true, anſwered I, that fine Ladies can be juſt what they pleaſe. You would be extremely in the wrong, if you hereafter complain of any Want of Sagacity in Phyſics. What you have been deſcribing is the very Method which the *Bologneſe* Philoſopher took; and by this Experiment he confirmed to his Fellow-Citizen the *Phoſphorus*, the Honour of ſhining by its own Light. It is probable that the innumerable other *Phoſphori* of the ſame Nature, lately diſcovered in *France*, owed their Luſtre to the ſame Cauſe: Theſe, by inriching Philoſophy with new Wonders, have deprived the *Bologneſe* of the Honour of Singularity, which is partook with only one other in the whole philoſophical World.

World. Do not Diamonds, the moſt valuable Phoſphorus of Nature, ſhine in the dark, becauſe the external Light kindles, and revives the internal Light, of which they are a rich and inexhauſtible Treaſure?

You may judge, replied the Marchioneſs, of my very great Sagacity in philoſophical Affairs, when I never obſerved a Phænomenon which I every Day carry about me. Perhaps, Madam, anſwered I, you were never in a Place dark enough to make this Obſervation. *Signore Boccari* one Day viſited a Lady in ſome Indiſpoſition, who was reſting behind a Screen far from the Air, and in a Place abſolutely dark. The Lady aſked him whether he had not a Light in his Hand; which he denied; but ſhe conſtantly inſiſting ſhe ſaw ſomething glitter, the Doctor at laſt ſuſpected it to be his Ring which ſhone in that profound Darkneſs, and perceived he had a long Time, without knowing it, carried a Phoſphorus upon his Finger. You may judge of the Value he afterwards ſet upon this Ring. He made innu-

innumerable Experiments with it about the Time that Mr. *Du Fay*, Father of so many Phosphori, found that Diamonds had the same Property. How empty and barren must the Philosophy of the Ancients have been, said the Marchioness, and how copious, how charming is ours, whose Observations enhance even the Value of Diamonds?

I will give you still greater Evidence, answered I, how much the Ancients were to blame in their Neglect of Experiments, and you will be fully convinced that there is none even of those which seem of least Importance, but what is of great Service to Natural Philosophy. That Froth we lately mentioned is an Instance of this, for as little philosophical as it may seem to vulgar Eyes, it was the principal Thing by which Sir *Isaac Newton* found out the Cause of those various and almost innumerable Colours which we see in Bodies.

He had discovered in general that certain Bodies appear of a certain Colour, because they reflect one

Sort

Sort of Rays more copiously than the rest, and other Bodies of different Colour, because they reflect a different Sort; so that if Light consisted of only one Sort of Rays, there could be only one Colour in the World, nor would it be possible by Refractions and Reflections to produce any new one.

This Discovery, which would perhaps have satisfied any other Philosopher, served only to excite the Curiosity of ours, and was but a Prelude to innumerable others.

Why should this Silk reflect the blue more freely than any other Sort of Rays? The Reason is this.

If one of those Bubbles which are formed by blowing Water a little thickened with Soap, be covered with Glass in order to prevent its being agitated by the Air, it will appear tinged with a great Variety of Colours, which spread themselves like so many Rings one within another, and incompass the Top of the Bubble. And in Proportion as the Bubble grows thinner by the continual subsiding of the Water, these Rings

slowly

ſlowly dilate and overſpread the whole, deſcending in order to the Bottom of it, where they all afterwards ſucceſſively vaniſh.

The Variety of theſe Colours depends on the unequal Thickneſs of the Bubble of Water in different Parts. But how to determine theſe Inequalities is not ſo eaſy, and perhaps would have been impoſſible to any but Sir *Iſaac Newton*, who examined theſe Rings a thouſand ways, guided by his conſtant Tutor Geometry, and a Spirit of Obſervation, whoſe Fertility ſeemed to increaſe in Proportion to the Difficulties it encountered.

He diſcovered that a certain determinate Thickneſs is neceſſary in a Plate of Water, (for Example) in order for it to reflect a particular Colour, and a different Thickneſs to make it reflect any other Colour, and in general, that a leſs Thickneſs is neceſſary to reflect the moſt refrangible Rays, as violet and indigo, than thoſe which are leaſt refrangible, as red and orange; all this is to be conſidered with Regard to a Subſtance

ſtance of equal Denſity. But when the Denſity in one Subſtance is leſs than in another, as the Denſity of Air compared with that of Water, a greater Thickneſs will be neceſſary in the firſt than in the laſt, to reflect the ſame Colour.

After the ſame Manner he defined the Thickneſſes neceſſary for the Tranſmiſſion of Colours. From the Analogy or Similitude between the Plates of Subſtances which he conſidered, and the Particles of which Bodies are compoſed, he demonſtrated that their Colours depend on nothing but the different Thickneſſes and Denſity in their Particles, whence it follows that ſome are more proper to reflect or tranſmit the Rays of one Colour, and others thoſe of a different one.

This Analogy holds good in many Inſtances. Thus the one and the other are tranſparent: The Leaves of Gold and the Particles of many other Bodies tranſmit one Colour and reflect another, juſt as the Bubbles of Water which we have been mentioning: Theſe Rings appear

appear of a various Colour when viewed in different Situations; the ſame happens in certain Silks, in the fine Web of the induſtrious Spider, and as *Taſſo* ſweetly ſings.

The Feathers ſo, that tender ſoft and plain
About the Dove's ſmooth Neck cloſe couched been,
Do in one Colour never long remain,
But change their Hew 'gainſt Glimpſe of Phœtus Sheen.
And now of Rubies bright a vermeil Chain,
Now make a Carknet rich of Emeralds green,
Now mingle both, now alter, turn, and change
To thouſand Colours rich, pure, fair, and ſtrange.

FAIRFAX's Taſſo.

This appears very evident in thoſe Powders that Painters make Uſe of, for when they are groun'd, (that is when their Parts are ſubtiliſed) their Colours change

change a little. Bodies may in ſome Meaſure be regarded as Stuffs, for their Threads, every one in particular reflecting a particular Sort of Rays, the whole Stuff appears of that Colour which is the Reſult of all the Rays reflected from the ſeveral Threads of which the Stuff is compoſed.

But what becomes of thoſe Rays which are not reflected? ſaid the Marchioneſs. Can you give an Account of them? They are either tranſmitted, anſwered I, or ſtifled and extinguiſhed, and are thus loſt among the Particles of Bodies. A Leaf of Gold placed between Light and the Eye is tranſparent, and appears of a greeniſh blue; but a Collection of theſe Leaves placed one upon another loſes both Colour and Tranſparency, the Rays which paſs thro' the firſt Leaf being abſolutely extinguiſhed in paſſing ſucceſſively thro' the reſt.

White Bodies (to continue our Similitude) are Stuffs compoſed of Threads which reflect all Colours; black, on the contrary, abſorb and extinguiſh every

Sort

Sort of Ray within themſelves. For this Reaſon black Bodies heat much more eaſily than any other; and a black Cap, ſuch as the *Engliſh* Ladies wear in St. *James*'s Park, would not at all agree with your Walks in the *Italian* Sun.

White Bodies as they reflect and drive every Sort of Ray from them, heat with more Difficulty than the others which imbibe and abſorb the Rays, and neither tranſmit or reflect them.

From the ſame Cauſes ariſe the various Colours which we diſcover in the Air. The different Denſity and Thickneſs of the Exhalations and Vapours that riſe from the Sea and Earth, paints the Heaven with varying Splendors, when roſy-fingered *Aurora* opens the Portals of the Morning, and calls back Mortals to their ſeveral Labours, or when *Veſper* invites them to an agreeable Repoſe; it is difficult however, to trace a Cauſe by which the Colours at the Riſing and Setting of the Sun are almoſt all the ſame, and ſucceed each other in a certain Order. But this we certainly know, that

that the ſeveral Colours of different Perſons Eyes proceeds from the Difference of Texture in the *Iris*, which is that Coat in the Eye that incompaſſes the Pupil.

The Variety of Fibres in the Iris kindles in ſome the imperious Look of a black Eye, in others the inſidious Sweetneſs of the blue. But it is not eaſy to aſſign a conſtant Cauſe why the Northern Nations ſhould generally have white Hair and blue or grey Eyes, and we of a warmer Imagination, not in a warmer Climate, ſhould have our Eyes black as our Hair.

This Syſtem however, will give us the Explication of a Phænomenon which is perhaps inexplicable in any other, and will thus make us a Compenſation for not being able to give a Reaſon for every thing in particular.

The Phænomenon is this: Two tranſparent Liquors, the one red and the other blue, ceaſe to be tranſparent when we look thro' both at the ſame Time. This Phænomenon which ſo greatly ſurpriſed the Perſon who firſt obſerved it, it, is only a Conſequence of the *Newtonian* Doctrine. The one of theſe Liquors tranſmits only red Rays, and the other only blue. Hence it follows, that the Rays tranſmitted by the one will be extinguiſhed and abſorbed by the other, and the Eye which looks through each of them receive none. And this Phænomenon is one of thoſe whoſe Explication becomes a Demonſtration of the Syſtem which is capable of explaining it.

That Opinion, ſaid the Marchioneſs, that blind People can diſtinguiſh Colours by their Feeling, now begins to appear credible to me: Or rather, is it not another Proof of our Syſtem? If our Feeling was finer than it is at preſent, as fine as that of blind Perſons perhaps is, could not we diſcover the Colour of a Body by feeling the different Thickneſs of its Particles? And thus we ſhould effect by our immediate Senſe, what a *Newtonian* would by his Calculations, if any one ſhould acquaint him with the hidden Texture of Bodies.

Your blind Obſervators, anſwered I, might

might diſtinguiſh Colours by their Feeling, even in the *Carteſian* Syſtem which you have now given up. For according to that, there muſt be a Difference in the Particles of Bodies of different Colours in order that the Rays of Light may be differently modified. A Proof like this you perceive is too ambiguous to deſerve a Place among thoſe we have already mentioned; and there is the ſame Defect in what is ſaid of a ſingular Kind of Barometer, which the *Chineſe* make Uſe of to form a Judgment of the Weather by. This Barometer is a Statue placed upon a Mountain, which foretels the Changes of the Sky and Air, by varying its own Colour.

But had we not better ſeek for a Phænomenon nearer ourelves in the Nation of Gallantry and Politeneſs, which can be explained by the *Engliſh* Syſtem alone? Why ſhould the Belles of that happy Country lay on more red when they appear in the Boxes at an Opera, than when they embelliſh with their Charms the agreeable Walks of the Thuilleries?

You

You lead Sir *Isaac Newton*'s System, said the Marchioness, into Places where you would have found it very difficult to lead its Author. Not if you, Madam, answered I, had been there.

The Light of a Candle is not so white as that of the Day; it has a yellowish Cast, and viewed thro' a Prism, yellow appears the most shining Colour in it. The less then the *Spanish* Wool is charged, or in other Words, the more it reflects other Rays besides the red, the stronger will the yellow appear, which is the predominant Colour in this Sort of Light; just as in a Chamber where the Light enters thro' coloured Curtains, the Objects in the Chamber will the more easily take the Colour of the Curtains in Proportion as their own Colour is weak and faint. This is evidently a Reason why the Quality of *Spanish* Wool should be augmented for the Opera, that neither the Cheeks of the Ladies, nor the Eyes of their Admirers may lose any thing, but find the same Advantages by the Light of the Evening as by that of the Day.

In

In the *Cartesian* Syſtem this wiſe Precaution would be entirely uſeleſs; for if the *Spaniſh* Wool can modify the Light of the Day, it would in the ſame manner modify that of the Evening, be it of what Colour it will.

Muſt it not be a Mortification, ſaid the Marchioneſs, for the Ladies of this happy Climate (if they ever have Time to conſider it) not to have a Syſtem in their own Country able to explain this Phænomenon in their Vermilion, but be obliged to call a foreign one from beyond Sea to their Aſſiſtance? So much the more glorious is it for this to extend its Empire over all Nations, even ſo far as to give them Leſſons for the Toilet. This is not the only one, anſwered I. If you would not have a blue appear green by Candle-Light (which might diſconcert the Harmony of a Suit of Cloaths, and cauſe innumerable Chagrins) you muſt be careful to chuſe it very clear, otherwiſe the blue Rays mixed with the yellow, which the Silk would reflect in greater Quantities by

Candle-

Candle-Light, might perhaps make it appear green.

These are the *Gordian* Knots of the Optic Science, which this System dissolves without eluding the Oracle. These Phænomena inexplicable to every other System, are without Difficulty explained in this. Every ambiguous Explication, every Proof that has not the Force of Demonstration, is intirely rejected by the *Newtonian* Philosophy.

An Analogy, for Instance, discovered between the Production of Colours and that of other Things, which would supply another System with a Proof, can serve only for Ornament and Luxury to this.

It has been lately discovered that Insects, Men, Animals and Plants, instead of being continually re-produced by Nature, only unfold themselves from their respective Plants or Seeds (in which they are really contained) whenever they find a proper Disposition for it; that is, both Animals and Plants wait for a proper Repository, certain Juices, Degrees of Heat, and other Things requisite to unfold

fold them. In the like Manner Colours are not, as was once believed, produced at every Refraction, or Reflection, or ſome other ſimilar Cauſe, but unfold themſelves, if I may uſe the Expreſſion, from the Boſom of Light, which contains them within itſelf, whenever it is refracted by a Priſm, or reflected from the Particles of Bodies. And this Method of their Production ſeems much more agreeable to the univerſal Laws and eſtabliſhed Order of Nature.

After the ſame Manner appears the Colour of the Rainbow, the coloured Circles ſometimes ſeen round the Sun and Moon, and thoſe of a certain Light, which is often ſeen towards the Northern Parts of Heaven, and called *Aurora Borealis*.

Whatever Riches and Magnificence, replied the Marchioneſs, Nature has diſplayed in ſo great a Variety of Colours, ſhe ſeems to have obſerved ſome Frugality in their Production. At leaſt the *Newtonian* Nature appears to me a better OEconomiſt than the *Carteſian*. The firſt has made Light a Magazine and Reſervoir of Colours, which ſhe produced once for all inſuſceptible of any Alteration, only with a certain Diſpoſition that renders them capable of being ſeparated from each other, and ſhewing us by this Separation a Colour, which all united and mixed together, they could not do; whereas the *Carteſian* Nature is every Moment obliged to give new Rotations to her Globules, and at every Refraction and every little Circumſtance, conſider in what Manner to vary them. This muſt be an infinite Fatigue to her, and a very great Application of Thought.

But theſe Diſpoſitions, anſwered I, which the Colours have to ſeparate themſelves, and which you ſo greatly admire, however convenient they may be to Nature by ſparing her ſo much Trouble and Thought, are ſometimes very inconvenient to us.

Inconvenient? replied the Marchioneſs. Is it not to theſe we are indebted for the beautiful Variety of the World? How tireſome and unpleaſant would it be for us to ſee in all Objects a Repetition

tition of the ſame Colour! You apprehend it, anſwered I, to be a great Evil always to ſee the World in *Chiaro oſcuro*, if I may uſe that Expreſſion, and to be obliged to be dreſſed always in the ſame Colour, and what is worſe, in a Colour like that of your own Complexion. You may add, replied ſhe, the Dread of loſing a Topic of Diſcourſe ſo very pleaſing to Ladies.

All theſe Misfortunes, anſwered I, and this terrible Addition of yours would happen, if the Rays had no Diſpoſition to ſeparate from each other, or if they were all of the ſame Colour. The *Cameleon* and wrinkled Faces would be conſiderable Loſers too. Some of theſe, without the Trouble of changing their Skin, are diſcovered in the Space of twelve, or at moſt twenty four Hours to change their Colours.

Aſtronomers on the other Hand would gain no ſmall Advantage if the Rays were inſeparable and of the ſame Colour. And what would not an Aſtronomer ſacrifice to determine the exact Time of an Eclipſe of *Jupiter*'s Satellites, or to get a diſtinct Sight of the Occultation of a Star by the Moon? Theſe are a Set of People whoſe Looks are always directed to Heaven, and have very little Regard for our Earth any farther than as ſhe is a Planet, and upon that Account enters into the cæleſtial Syſtem. This is all they regard in her, and therefore would feel very little Concern if the Ladies of this Planet were under an Impoſſibility of changing every Day the Colour of their Cloaths, or ſubject to many other the like Inconveniencies.

But what Oppoſition, replied the Marchioneſs, can there be betwixt the Separability of the coloured Rays and the Obſervations of theſe Gentlemen, to make them quarrel with us for the Pleaſure we receive from this Variety? There is a very great Oppoſition betwixt them, anſwered I, and you will be ſoon convinced of it, when I tell you that the Separability of the Rays is prejudicial to the Perfection of Teleſcopes, which Aſtronomers regard as their very Eyes. I before poſitively affirmed that Con-

Convex-Glaſſes, of which Teleſcopes are compoſed, unite the Rays, which proceeding from a Point, fall upon them into another Point. But the Truth is, I ſpoke rather with Regard to what they ſhould do than what they really do. You ſeem, ſaid the Marchioneſs, to have repreſented theſe Glaſſes in the ſame Light as tragic Writers do their Heroes; for theſe generally chuſe to feign them what they ought to be, rather than imitate their Characters ſuch as they really are.

It muſt be confeſſed, Madam, that I uſed a Sort of poetic Licence in telling you Convex-Glaſſes united the Rays into a Point, for it is not ſo truly a Point as a little Circle. This Circle, which is called the *Abberration* of the *Light*, proceeds from two Cauſes, the Figure commonly given to the Lens, and that Diſpoſition which the Rays of Light have to ſeparate themſelves when they are refracted. But indeed the Figure of the Lens is but a very ſmall Obſtacle when compared to that of the different Refrangibility. All attempts therefore to render Telescopes more perfect by giving a new Figure to the Lens, so as to make it unite the Rays truly in a Point, would be in vain.

In the Golden Age, of which the Poets give us so many fine Descriptions, when the Rivers flowed with Milk, and the Oaks distilled the fragrant Treasure of the Bee, when the Rams appeared in the Meadows arrayed in native Purple, and the Lamb displayed its vivid Scarlet to the Sun, before the Hand of Art had taught the Fleeces to imitate different Dies: In these happy Times, tis probable, the Telescope would have given a more distinct View of the Objects of Nature herself painted in their genuine and beauteous Colours, when the Heart of Man, animated with purer Passions, appeared without Disguise, and Love had not yet learned to sigh by Custom or Art, nor ever wept from any Motive but Joy. But in our Iron Age, in which both the Passions and Colours have degenerated from their original Purity, whatever be the Figure of the

Lens,

Lens, the Point where the blue or green Rays unite, will always be different from that of the yellow and red; there muſt always be an Abberration of the Light; and that little Circle will never become a Point. This is a Circum ſtance very inconvenient for Aſtronomers, whoſe Affairs require that every thing ſhould be ſeen extremely diſtinct; but this Circle where the Rays unite inſtead of the Point where they ought to unite, or the different Refrangibility, which is the Cauſe of their uniting thus irregularly, is a great Obſtacle to the obtaining the Exactneſs which Aſtronomers deſire.

These accurate Gentlemen, ſaid ſhe, muſt have Patience, and pray for the Return of the Golden Age. In the mean Time they muſt limit their Deſires and Wants as other reaſonable Men do, and be contented with the different Refrangibility of the Rays inſtead of that very great Diſtinctneſs in Objects which they deſire. It is not poſſible to have all Things at one Time in this World. Is the Knowledge of ſo many fine and ſurpriſing Properties of Light ſo very ſmall an Acquirement, that they cannot be ſatisfied without ſomething more? Their Deſires and their Wants however are ſo reaſonable, ſaid I, and have ſo great a Connexion with thoſe of other People, that Sir *Iſaac Newton* has thought upon a Method of ſatisfying them. With his own Hand he ground Glaſſes for Teleſcopes of a new Figure, in order to correct the Deficiency of ordinary Lenſes. Then was the Time to have All, or hereafter hope for Nothing.

While his Mind was imployed in this Thought a new Scene of Optics opened to his View, he diſcovered the different Refrangibility of the Rays, laid aſide the Work he had begun, and invented a new Teleſcope, in which a poliſhed Minor ſupplies the Place of what in ordinary Teleſcopes is called the Object-Glaſs, and which had the greateſt Share in the Abberration of Light.

I myſelf have ſeen the firſt Teleſcope of this Sort, worked by thoſe Hands which had pointed to the Planets their Road

Road in the vaſt Deſarts of a Vacuum, and opened to Geometry the immenſe Carier of Infinity. This Inſtrument is preſerved in a City of *England* where Philoſophy and Politeneſs hold a mutual Empire; with this are treaſured up thoſe Priſms which the firſt Time differently refracted the Rays of Light in the Hands of our Great Philoſopher, ſeparated its Emeralds, Hyacinths and Rubies, and unfolded to human Eyes the celeſtial Riches of the lucid Robe of Day.

In the Reflection from a Mirror the Rays are not ſeparated as they are in being refracted thro' a Lens, conſequently the Objects may be much more diſtinctly ſeen.

It has been tried in *Italy* (for even among us Truth and Sir *Iſaac Newton* have their Admirers) that if a diſtant Object, the one Half red and the other blue, be viewed with an ordinary Teleſcope, this Inſtrument muſt be conſiderably ſhortened to give a diſtinct Sight of the blue Half, and on the contrary muſt be lengthened to ſhew the red diſtinctly; whereas in Sir *Iſaac Newton*'s Teleſcope they appear equally diſtinct with the ſame Length.

This reflecting Teleſcope has beſides another Advantage over the ordinary ones, for one of Sir *Iſaac*'s Invention one Foot long is equivalent to one of twelve in the common Sort; and one of forty Foot, to a hundred. And this is another Convenience to Aſtronomers who find great Difficulty in managing long Teleſcopes.

It is well for us, replied the Marchioneſs, that theſe Aſtronomers will be now contented, for it ſeemed before a pretty difficult Matter to pleaſe them. How is it poſſible, anſwered I, for them not to be ſatisfied with Sir *Iſaac Newton*, who ſeems in every Thing to have ſtudied their Advantage?

His Syſtem of Optics (beſides procuring them a more convenient and perfect Teleſcope) has vindicated the Honour of Aſtronomy from an Aſperſion, which ſeemed in ſome Meaſure to diſgrace it in the Eyes of the World. You are not ignorant that the Honour of of this Science among Men consists principally in its exact Prediction of Eclipses and Events, no less observable to philosophical than to vulgar Eyes. *Thales* of *Miletus* was reverenced among the *Greeks* like a God for having predicted the Year in which an Eclipse of the Sun was to happen, that is, when the Moon would be interposed betwixt us and the Sun, and by that means deprive us of his Light.

As Astronomy successively became more perfect, what would have caused a Temple to be erected to a *Thales*, would only disgrace a *Hally*, *Cassini*, or a *Manfredi*.

The Observatory is required to shew the precise Minute in which the Eclipse will happen, and its exact Quantity, or in other Words, whether the Moon will observe the whole Sun or only a Part, and how much precisely the obscured Part will be.

Not long since all the Calculations of the most celebrated Astronomers had predicted two total Eclipses, whose principal Merit consists in not being very common, and in introducing a ſudden and unſeaſonable Night. An Event which tho' foretold and expected, never fails to terrify that whimſical Species of Animals called Man, that *Azylum* of the ſtrongeſt Contradictions, nouriſhed by long Hopes, impetuous Paſſions, the moſt evident Truth and the moſt palpable Error, capable of making Attempts beyond the Powers of his Nature, and ſubject to Fears which his Reaſon contradicts.

All the Philoſophers got up very early on the Days appointed for this Spectacle, in order to prepare themſelves for Obſervation. They all waited in the Midſt of the Eclipſe to ſee the Light of the Sun entirely extinguiſhed, and a moſt gloomy and profound Night emerge from the Splendor of a fine Day. But the Event was contrary to their Expectations. There remained round the Moon a luminous Ring which made ſome falſly take them for annular Eclipſes. When the Sun is neareſt to the Earth, and the Moon at the greateſt poſſible Diſtance, if there happens

happens in theſe Circumſtances a Central Eclipſe, as they call it, the Moon cannot hide all the Sun, but there remains all round its Edge a luminous Border reſembling a Ring. But Aſtronomers gained nothing by this Explication, which was of no Signification in the preſent Caſe, and the World was but ill ſatisfied with Aſtronomy which is now believed an Impoſtor. The one murmured and were diſcontented, while the other racked their Brains to find the Reaſon of this Ring, which had the Confidence to appear in Spite of all their Calculations.

Some laid the Fault upon a luminous Atmoſphere which incompaſſes the Sun, as our Air does the Earth, and became viſible when the greater Light was obſcured; others accuſed the Atmoſphere of the Moon, which being illuminated at the Time of the Eclipſe, appeared like a lucid Ring. But unhappily for them the firſt was innocent, and the ſecond ſeemed ſo doubtful, that it might appear rather

rather a Mark of their Consternation, than an Explication of the Phænomenon.

I find myself greatly affected with Concern, said the Marchioness, for these unfortunate Astronomers abandoned by Heaven and Earth, and in the utmost Danger of losing their Reputation. It is however the Office of Humanity to have Compassion on the Afflicted. They must have Recourse, answered I, to the *Newtonian* Oracles if they would silence the Voice of Calumny. These were the Anchor of Hope in the present calamitous State of Affairs.

When the Rays of Light pass near the Extremity of a Body, they bend and incline towards the Body itself, and are thrown into its Shadow. If the Edge of a Knife be placed in a Ray of Light in a dark Chamber, the Rays which pass at some Distance from it, appear to bend and approach nearer its Back. *Grimaldo* was the first who observed this Quality which is called the *Diffraction* or *Inflection* of Light, and our Philosopher afterwards illustrated

it

it with many new Experiments; and tho' he did a great deal, desired to do still more.

The solar Rays which pass near the Edges of the Moon must bend and cast themselves into the Shadow of the Moon herself. Observers then, who in the Time of an Eclipse are immersed in this Shadow, must receive these Rays bent from the Edges of the Moon, and see a luminous Ring round her, a Sort of Twilight resembling that which we see in the Evening and sometimes in the Morning, at the Horizon. The only Difference between our Twilight and this Ring is, that the first is occasioned by the Refraction which the Light suffers in coming from the Celestial Spaces into our Air, and the second by the *Diffraction* which it undergoes in passing near the Moon: But both are composed of Rays which do not seem destined by Nature for that Purpose.

To give a stronger Confirmation that this is the true Reason of this Ring, there have been made several Globes of artificial Moons, which exposed to the Sun

Sun and full Moon, have ſhown upon Earth the Effects of that Diffraction which had appeared ſo fatal to Aſtronomy in Heaven.

Aſtronomers, replied the Marchioneſs, have certainly great Reaſon to be ſatisfied with Sir *Iſaac Newton* and his *Diffraction*, which has delivered them from ſuch eminent Danger. But I muſt confeſs myſelf to be yet throughly diſcontented with it. Will you permit me to aſk why thoſe Rays which paſs at ſome Diſtance from Bodies, muſt be inflected and bent? The Idea which this new Property of Light preſents me with, is ſo very ſtrange that I cannot conceive it. I find, anſwered I, you are more difficult to ſatisfy than the Aſtronomers themſelves. You deſire to know the Cauſe of this *Diffraction*. Well, I'll inform you, but you muſt promiſe not to draw back and frown when I tell you it is the Attraction which Bodies exerciſe upon Light. The Attraction! ſaid the Marchioneſs with an Air of Surprize. You ſay this either to laugh at my Credulity, or puniſh my

too

too presumptuous Curiosity. What, do Bodies attract the Light as a Loadstone does Iron? What ill Consequences would arise supposing it were so? answered I, Or rather how great an Advantage has the Science of Optics in particular gained from this Attraction between Light and Bodies, as all Natural Philosophy in general has from the universal Attraction of Matter, of which that between Bodies and Light is a Consequence?

Attraction is the Key of all Philosophy, the great Spring that actuates the Frame of Nature; the universal and mysterious Force discovered and calculated by Sir *Isaac Newton*, proposed to the Examination of Philosophers by the great Lord *Bacon*, and obscurely sung by the *British Homer*.

The Marchioness recollected herself, and looked very attentively in my Face to see whether I spoke in Earnest. Do you tell me seriously, she replied, that all Bodies are attracted? This is quite a new World to me when I am an utter Stranger and Foreigner. Do not be dis-

discouraged, said I, for this has happened to many professed Philosophers who have exclaimed against this Attraction, affirming, that to admit it is introducing into Philosophy certain occult Qualities which the Ancients supposed in Bodies, such as Sympathy, Antipathy and the like, whose Numbers multiplied with the Phænomena themselves, by the Assistance of which they in an Instant explained, or rather perplexed every Thing.

They farther add, that it is recalling those occult Qualities from those Colleges of *Europe*, where Ignorance still affords them an Asylum to introduce them into true Philosophy, from whence they for the Happiness of Mankind had been banished by the Authority of Reason.

But all these Objections signify nothing, for Attraction is so far from being an *occult*, that it is an extremely *evident* Quality of Matter, on which clearly depends the Explication of *Diffraction*, Refraction itself, and innumerable other Things. It is not a Name without Reality, invented to explain

two

two or three Appearances, but a general Principle diffused thro' all Nature, and extends from the smallest Grain of Sand to the greatest Planet. The *Peripatetics* resembled those Ancients, who for every little River or Tree, nay even for the Fever or the Cholic, created a new Deity. But Sir *Isaac Newton* appears as a great Philosopher, who by the Help of Attraction establishes the Existance of an all-powerful, infinite and only God, the Supreme Director of the whole Frame of Nature.

Sir *Isaac Newton* (when he affirms that Light in passing near the Extremity of Bodies is attracted by them, does not pretend by that to give a compleat Explication of *Diffraction*; all he undertakes is only to point out that Property of Matter on which the Explication of *Diffraction* depends, but the Cause of this Property is to seek. This he commits to those Philosophers who have superfluous Time enough to throw away in Search of a Thing which appears above the Reach of human Faculties. In short, all that Sir

Isaac

Iſaac Newton attempts is to eſtabliſh Facts and the general Properties of Matter, and from theſe geometrically to deduce Phænomena and Effects; and this is the Order we have hitherto obſerved in our Diſcourſe upon Light and Colours.

This new Property, replied the Marchioneſs, is of a Nature which my Thoughts cannot ſo eaſily come into. This is one of thoſe hiſtorical Facts of which it is impoſſible to get a perfect Intelligence without entering into the Cabinet. I underſtand, or think I underſtand, how the Rays of Light are differently refrangible. This, among many other Things, is very intelligible. But that Bodies ſhould attract the Light, and that at a certain Diſtance too, and in general that every thing ſhould be mutually attracted, ſeems to me very difficult to conceive.

Some Remains of *Carteſianiſm*, anſwered I, which you are not yet entirely free from, deceives you in this Point. Perhaps you have hitherto flattered your-

yourself that Refraction arises from some one of those Causes which in treating upon the *Cartesian* System were rendered so familiar to you, and upon this Account you think Refraction more intelligible than *Diffraction.* Sir *Isaac Newton* himself appears in some Places to have indulged the Prejudices of this Sect. In order to speak the Language then current in Philosophy, he said, that Attraction perhaps might be the Impulse of a subtile Matter proceeding from Bodies. But in Fact after he had proved the Heavens to be empty, and the Celestial Bodies mutually attracted in those vast Spaces, what Room did there remain for the Impulse and subtile Matter? He seems to resemble certain Authors, who, to make their History agreeable to any particular Nation, are sometimes obliged to intersperse it with fabulous Episodes, and give it the Air of a Romance. Is it not a great Reproach upon Mankind that even the Truths of Sir *Isaac Newton* were obliged to use some little Artifice

in

in order to meet with a Reception among them?

Is not this rather an Artifice of yours, interrupted the Marchioneſs, to ſurprize me by a Motive of Honour, and in this Manner make me believe that I have no better Conception of the ſubtile Matter than of Attractions, or how Bodies ſhould be indued with Motion, for Example, than with that which you rightly term a *myſterious* Force?

Your Illuſion, anſwered I, proceeds from hence, that you are familiarized to one Idea and not to the other. You every Day ſee Bodies move and mutually communicate their Motion, but you have never ſeen them *attract* each other. You are ſurprized at Attraction while Motion appears to have no Difficulty. In this you differ from Philoſophers who like Poets for the Solution of any difficult Point are obliged to have Recourſe to the Divinity for the Explications both of Motion and its Communication.

A *Portugueſe* accuſtomed to reverence Spectacles upon the Noſe of the graveſt

graveſt Perſons as a Mark of the greateſt Dignity, would probably be ſurprized to ſee a *Chineſe* Mandarin let his Nails grow to an enormous Length for the very ſame Reaſon. And the Cauſe of his being ſurprized in one Caſe and not in the other is, that a long Habit has connected in his Mind the two Ideas of Honour and Spectacles which have nothing in common with each other, but has not connected thoſe of Honour and long Nails. I ſhall at leaſt deſerve more Compaſſion than the *Portugueſe*, replied the Marchioneſs, becauſe the Surpriſe of ſeeing Matter united to Attraction inſtead of Motion will I believe be common to all Countries.

As univerſal and excuſable as this Surpriſe may be, I anſwered, it muſt however at laſt ſubmit to Reaſon. If you had never ſeen Bodies move it would have been impoſſible for you to gueſs how Motion would be joined with Extenſion and mutual Impenetrability, which would be all the Qualities you would then have been acquainted with. It is Obſervation which has made you admit

admit this Property in Matter, and Obſervation muſt make you allow Attraction. We are as yet but Children in this vaſt Uuiverſe, and are very far from having a compleat Idea of Matter; we are utterly unable to pronounce what Properties are agreeable to it, and what are not. We ſee Bodies in very near the ſame Manner as a Perſon who ſhould receive his Senſes by little and little. It would certainly be great Temerity in him to affirm that there cannot be a Property in Matter capable of moving the Eye, and ſhould aſſign as a Reaſon for this Aſſertion, that he had never been able to obſerve any ſuch Property.

This Perſon would not act like the *Carteſians* who form a World and a Man juſt as their own Caprice directed them; he would grow more cautious in limiting the Power of Nature and pronouncing the Qualities of Bodies, in Proportion as he ſhould acquire new Senſes, which would every Day furniſh him with freſh Diſcoveries of theſe Things.

Phi-

Philoſophers may be ſaid in ſome Degree to acquire new Senſes, or rather thoſe they before had become every Day more refined, and are by that Means in a Capacity of perceiving what perhaps they had once no Idea of. Hence it evidently follows, how very cautiouſly they ought to proceed in aſſigning the Number of Properties in Matter. It ſignifies nothing to ſay that ſome are more intelligible than others, for to ſpeak ingenuouſly, they are all equally myſterious to us.

Will you any longer make a Difficulty, Madam, to admit Attraction as a Property of Matter when it is proved ſo many Ways, and principally by the heavenly Phænomena, which give the moſt ſhining Teſtimony to a Thing that you yourſelf ſo evidently demonſtrate the Truth of? I aſſure you for my Part I ſhall never look for any farther Demonſtration of it than what you afford.

But I, replied the Marchioneſs, ſhall not be ſo eaſily ſatisfied, for I have need of the daily Atteſtation of all Heaven itſelf to convince me of a Thing which yet appears ſo ſtrange and ſurpriſing. It is abſolutely needful then, continued I, to give you a full Conviction of it. And indeed it would be doing a great Injury both to Sir *Iſaac Newton* and yourſelf, to endeavour to make you believe a Thing without giving you good Reaſons. I am ſorry this Syſtem cannot be explained to you with all the Force of thoſe Demonſtrations and Calculations which accompany it; without theſe you muſt certainly loſe a great deal. I will have Patience, ſaid ſhe; if I cannot ſee it in all that Luſtre in which it would appear to a Mathematician, and will act like thoſe Virtuoſi, who when they cannot get a Picture content themſelves with the Copy of it. I flatter myſelf you will render it as like the Original as poſſible. It is at preſent too late, I replied, for this Expedition. To-morrow we will aſcend into Heaven, and from thence bring Attraction down in Triumph to Earth. Some Aſtronomical Facts and Propoſitions in Geometry, which you may ſafely

ſafely believe upon the Word of Sir *Iſaac Newton*, ſhall ſerve for a Hippo-gryph, or flying Car, to tranſport us to the Skies.

The SIXTH DIALOGUE.

Expoſition of the Newtonian *univerſal Principle of Attraction, and Application of this Principle to Optics.*

CONCLUSION.

THE next Morning the Marchioneſs no leſs impatient for Attraction than ſhe had been for all the reſt, after a few ſhort Compliments, began, It is now Time to mount our Hippogryph, and give him the Reins. He will not grow weary, anſwered I, for a little Journey, if I can remember certain horrible Numbers.

All the Planets revolve at various Diſtances round the Sun, who is almoſt nine hundred thouſand Times bigger than the Earth, and forms the Centre of their Motion, while he remains in the

the Tranquillity of a Majeſtic Repoſe. Neareſt the Sun, at a Diſtance however of thirty-two Millions of *Engliſh* Miles, is the little World of *Mercury*, then follows the lucid Orb of *Venus* fifty nine Millions diſtant, then our Earth eighty one, *Mars* at one hundred and twenty three, the enormous Bulk of *Jupiter* four hundred and twenty four, and the vaſt and ſlow-moving *Saturn*, ſeven hundred and ſeventy ſeven Millions of Miles.

Theſe all preſerve this natural Order in their Motions, that thoſe neareſt the Sun compleat their Revolution or Orbit in a ſhorter Time, and the moſt diſtant in a longer: Thus *Mercury* finiſhes his Revolution in eighty eight Days, *Venus* in two hundred and twenty four and ſome Hours, the Earth, as you already know, in a Year, *Mars* in about two Years, *Jupiter* in almoſt twelve, and *Saturn* in about twenty nine Years and a Half.

There is ſo great a Dependance and Relation between the periodical Revolutions of the Planets and their Diſtances from the Sun, that if we know the Diſtances of any two (of the Earth and *Jupiter* for Inſtance) and the periodical Time of one, (ſuppoſe of the Earth) by a certain Rule we may find the periodical Time of the other.

I ſhould have a much clearer Idea of your Meaning, ſaid the Marchioneſs, if I had firſt read *Fontenelle*'s Plurality of Worlds to convince me of the Motion and Agility of the Earth. As you are now ſo great a Proficient in Philoſophy, I replied, you muſt ſeek the true Demonſtration of this Motion in *England*.

There have been obſerved certain Appearances in the Stars which ſome imagined to be Conſequences of this Motion, but others who examined it more ſtrictly, have diſcovered theſe Appearances to be contrary to the Laws of ſuch a Motion. The Motion of Light which is a conſiderable Time in coming from the Stars to us muſt ſtrangely vary their Appearances, and ought to be conſidered in Conjunction with the Earth's Motion round the Sun, in order

to

to give a right Deciſion of the Queſtion.

The Sagacity of the *Engliſh* Philoſophers has in Fact united theſe two Motions, and by this Means they explain theſe ſurprizing and various Appearances which in any other Syſtem are abſolutely inexplicable. And thus we have attained to the Certainty of a Thing proved a thouſand Ways, but never ſtrictly demonſtrated by any.

The five Planets in whoſe Number we may ſafely replace our Earth, are called *Primary*, to diſtinguiſh them from other ſubaltern Planets which revolve round a Primary as the Moon does round our Earth, the four Satellites of *Jupiter* round that Planet, and five round *Saturn*; and theſe Sabalterns are called *Secondaries*. Theſe laſt agree with their Primaries in obſerving this Order, that the neareſt compleat their Orbit in a leſs, and the moſt diſtant in a greater Time; and they keep this Law with the ſame Exactneſs and the ſame Relation as their Primaries do.

Another Law in which the primary and ſecondary Planets agree is, that they do not deſcribe equal Parts of Orbits in equal Times, but ſuch Parts of Orbits as to make their Areas equal. That you may better underſtand this other Law of their Motion, you are to ſuppoſe that the Orbit of a primary Planet is very near a Circle which the Sun is not placed directly in the Center of, but a little on one Side. Imagine a Line to be drawn from that Point of the Orbit where the Planet now is, to the Sun, and another Line to be drawn from that Point where the Planet will be twenty four Hours hence. The Space contained betwixt the two Lines drawn to the Sun, and that Part of the Orbit which the Planet has deſcribed in twenty four Hours, is called the *Area*, and will be equal to another ſuch Area, that the Planet will deſcribe in twenty four Hours more; and thus in equal Times the Areas will be always equal.

The *Areas* then, as Aſtronomers expreſs it, are *proportional to the Times.* Thus if inſtead of twenty four Hours we put twelve, which is one Half, an Area deſcribed in thoſe twelve Hours will be

only

only one Half of the Area deſcribed in the 24; and ſo, if we take a third or fourth part of the Time, the Areas deſcribed in that third or fourth Part, will be the third or fourth of thoſe deſcribed in the firſt Time; and if that Time be doubled, the Area deſcribed in it will be doubled likewiſe, and ſo on. This Law which the primary Planets obſerve with Regard to the Sun, the ſecondary Planets obſerve with Regard to the Primary, round which they revolve; and this Primary is the ſame to its Satellites, as the Sun is to the Planets of the firſt Order.

I am extremely pleaſed, ſaid the Marchioneſs, with the Agreement between theſe two Sorts of Planets. I regard the Sun as Monarch of the immenſe planetary Realm, in which the primary Planets are the Grandees and Nobles; ſome of theſe poſſeſs certain Diſtricts, where they exerciſe the ſame Juriſdiction in little which their Sovereign does in great, but all ſhew their Dependance by revolving round him alone.

Our Earth is in Poſſeſſion of a little Province, where ſhe exacts Obedience from the Moon; and tho' ſhe cannot vie with *Jupiter* or *Saturn* who have a greater Number of Dependants, ſhe is certainly ſuperior to *Mars*, *Mercury* and *Venus*, who have none.

Your Similitude, anſwered I, would be juſter in the *Carteſian* Syſtem of Vortices where theſe Juriſdictions ſeem very well eſtabliſhed; and it would be the more ſo, becauſe this philoſophical Poetry is fond of imbelliſhing itſelf with Compariſons and Similies, and ſometimes makes them even ſerve for Reaſons. But the two Laws I have mentioned to you, will not ſuffer it. Indeed it is Pity we are obliged to abandon theſe Vortices, that preſent the Mind with ſo clear, ſo natural and ſimple an Idea. The Planets, ſay the *Carteſians*, revolve round the Sun, becauſe a certain Fluid in which they are immerſed turns round too, and carries them with it like little Skiffs forced along by the Current of a River. The ſecondary Planets revolve round their Primaries for the ſame Reaſon.

Nothing ſeems to be more evident than this. But the Misfortune is that

theſe

these Planets are not contented with barely turning round, but will do it by certain inviolable Laws that intirely destroy all these imaginary Systems.

Either these two Laws cannot agree with the Vortices, or agree so ill, notwithstanding all the Efforts to that Purpose, that one of their most illustrious Defenders confesses, after all he has done in their Support, he doubted whether those who refuse to admit them would not be confirmed in their Opinion by the very Manner in which he has endeavoured to defeat it. Besides these Vortices are pressed by so many other insuperable Difficulties, that Heaven itself seems to have conspired in the Destruction of this fine Poem.

Far be it from us, replied the Marchioness, to oppose the Decrees of Heaven. On the other Hand, I cannot reconcile myself to the Idea of a Poem in Philosophy. What is this philosophical Poetry to which I cannot assign a Place in my Thoughts? It ought to content itself with influencing the Passions of *Men*, but it has nothing to do with the single Passion of *Philosophers*, which is Truth.

The *Newtonian* Principles, anſwered I, have inſpired you with very rigid Sentiments. But this Poetry, that thinks itſelf too much limited in the vaſt Field of human Paſſions, ſhall give you no further Trouble. Comets, the moſt declared Enemies in all Heaven to their Vortices, will I believe be ſufficient to overthrow it, for they ſeem to be made expreſly for the Deſtruction of Syſtems.

It has been eſtabliſhed, by Virtue of I know not what, but however the Philoſophers have very readily believed, that the Matter of the Heavens was incorruptible, and that every thing there flouriſhed in a perpetual Youth, inſuſceptible of the Changes and Viciſſitudes which happen here below. The Comets appear at firſt almoſt naked, but in their Approach to the Sun are cloathed with a formidable Tail, of which they gradually diveſt themſelves as they recede from him, and ſo return back naked as they came. And in this Manner is the Syſtem of the Incorruptibility of Heavenly Regions, in great Danger of being overthrown by theſe impertinent Comets. And this perhaps is the Reaſon why they were degraded from their Celeſtial Seat as worthleſs Meteors formed by the Vapours and Exhalations of our lower World. But they would not remain long there; for beſides many ancient Philoſophers who conſidered them not as one of the tranſient, but durable Works of Nature, the Aſtronomers who muſt have their Share in a Thing above us, aſſure us, that they are very diſtant from the Earth, and ſome of them farther off than the Sun himſelf. Theſe Comets, ſaid the Marchioneſs, are very bad Omens to Syſtems, if not to crowned Heads. Theſe were not all the Troubles, ſaid I, which they gave Philoſophers. When they were placed among the celeſtial Bodies, they could not agree with that Solidity which had been granted to the Heavens upon the Word of *Ariſtotle*; in order therefore to avoid their demoliſhing and breaking to Pieces the whole Univerſe in their Paſſage through theſe *Ariſtotelian* Heavens, it was neceſſary to reſolve upon making theſe laſt fluid.

When the Heavens were thus made fluid they became Vortices, againſt which

which these factious Comets renewed their Enmity with more Violence than ever, to destroy an agreeable Imagination received by the World with so much Applause, and which was defective in nothing but Truth.

Some Comets have made no Difficulty to cross the Orbits of all the Planets, proceeding almost directly from the superior Part of the Vortex to the Sun; others have moved in a Course absolutely contrary to that of the Planets, without meeting either in the first or second Case, any Resistance in their Motion, which must necessarily have happened, if there was a certain Matter that whirl'd round the Sun, and this at several Distances from him with the same Rapidity as the Planets supposed to swim in those Vortices. Their Motion would have been so weakened, that turning round the same Way as the Planets do, they would soon have yielded to the irresistible Force of the Vortices, not unlike the unfortunate Barks, which guided by an unskilful Pilot or a malignant Star, are Ship-wreck'd in the horrible Cata-

racts

racts of the *Chinese* Rivers, notwithstanding all the struggling they can make to the contrary.

In short, these Comets have in every Instance acted directly opposite to the Laws of Vortices. So that to rescue them from the continual Injuries they receive from these implacaable Enemies which lay hold on every Occasion to commit all Sorts of Hostility and Impertinence, I see no other Remedy than to destroy and banish these unhappy Fluids for ever from the System of the World.

Your Expedient, replied the Marchioness, is no less violent than that sometimes used in War, when one Party destroy and ruin a Country which they cannot defend against the Enemy. And thus they make the same Sacrifice to their Weakness as you do to Truth. This is a Sacrifice at which I cannot be displeased, especially as it puts me into a better Capacity of listening with more Tranquillity to the new Principle upon which the celestial System is built.

Sir *Isaac Newton*, continued I, founded his Scheme in Geometry, which we

ma-

may call his native Country. He began with demonſtrating that if a Body in Motion is attracted towards a Point either moveable or immoveable, it will deſcribe about this Point equal Areas in equal Times, and in general, that the Areas will be proportional to the Times; and on the contrary, if a Body deſcribes round a moveable or immoveable Point Areas proportional to the Times, it will be attracted towards that Point, that is, the Body will have ſuch a Tendency towards the Point, that if every other Motion which impels it a different Way ſhould ceaſe, the Body would directly unite itſelf to that Point, juſt as Bodies here below, when left to themſelves, fall directly upon the Earth.

This Principle, interrupted the Marchioneſs, is equally applicable both to the primary and ſecondary Planets. Each of theſe deſcribe Areas proportional to the Times, round the Point about which they turn (if the Sun, our Earth and *Jupiter* may be termed Points). The primary Planets then are attracted by the Sun, and the ſecondary

by

by their respective Primaries about which they revolve. Is not this a necessary Consequence? It is without Dispute absolutely necessary, answered I. But remember, Madam, this is a Deduction of your own. This Punishment is just, since you have made so much Difficulty to admit the Principle of Attraction.

You say then that there is a Force in the Sun which attracts the Planets to him, and after the same Manner, a Force in the Planets that attracts the Satellites, and this attractive Force joined with another by which they all move from West to East, is the Reason why the first revolve round the Sun, and the others round their Primaries, in a certain Order.

The Ancients, in order to explain this difficult Phænomenon, built solid Heavens and created Intelligences to put them in Motion; on the other Hand, *Des Cartes* had imbarassed the whole Universe with the great and magnificent Apparatus of his Vortices. But after all, the Motion of the heavenly Bodies is by Sir *Isaac Newton* reduced to the most simple yet the most noble

Phæ-

Phænomenon in the World, which has been rendered much more familiar in *Europe*, than is agreeable to ſome Perſons. In ſhort it is no more than that of a Bullet, which would of itſelf proceed in a direct Line, if the attractive Force of the Earth did not oblige it to move in a Curve. The Bullet very ſoon falls to the Earth, becauſe the greateſt Force we can poſſibly give it, is but little when compared to the vaſt Extent of this Globe. If it were poſſible for human Weakneſs to throw one from hence beyond *Peru*, it is demonſtrated that we ſhould acquire a new Satellite; it would like the Moon revolve about our Earth, only its Motion being neceſſarily very ſoon weakened from the continual Reſiſtance of the Air, while the gravitating Force would loſe nothing of its Strength, this new Moon would at laſt fall and deſtroy every thing it lighted on, after we had heard it make a horrible hiſſing over our Heads.

All this you explain in two Sentences; an evident Proof of the Significancy of a Lady's Words. What you have ſaid is certainly a great deal, but not all. It ſtill remains to know by what Law this attractive Force acts, that is, whether it be the ſame at all Diſtances from the Sun, or whether it grows weaker in Proportion as the Diſtance is greater. I will reſolve you this Queſtion, the Marchioneſs replied, when you have furniſhed me with as many Hints for that Purpoſe as you did when I told you that the Planets are attracted by the Sun; and I hope you will afterwards make as genteel a Commentary upon me as you did in the other Caſe.

That Law, anſwered I, of deſcribing Areas proportional to the Times obſerved by every particular Planet, furniſhed Sir *Iſaac Newton* with Means to diſcover the attractive Force of the Sun; and that other Law which they obſerve, of deſcribing their Orbits in a greater Time in Proportion as they are at a greater Diſtance from the Sun, and that with a certain Relation between theſe Times and their Diſtances, helped him to find out that the attractive Force diminiſhes

miniſhes as the Diſtance from the Sun increaſes.

The attractive Force diminiſhes with this Proportion, that it is always ſo much leſs as the Square of the Number which expreſſes the Diſtance from the Sun is greater. In order to underſtand this Cyphering (which perhaps at firſt Sight may appear very formidable) it is neceſſary to acquaint you that the *Square* of any Number is nothing but that ſame Number multiplied by itſelf, as *four* for Inſtance is the Square of *two*, becauſe *twice two* makes *four*, that is, *two* multiplied by itſelf gives *four*.

I may now ſafely venture to propoſe you a Problem, that as you have lately explained the Phænomena of Natural Philoſophy, you may now undertake the Solution of mathematical Problems: After this I do not ſee what you can do better than to ſhew ſome Sort of Gratitude, and diſcover the Truth to him who has conducted you into its moſt abſtruſe and retired Paths.

The Problem I ſhall propoſe to you is this: Suppoſe the Earth's Diſtance from

from the Sun to be *one*, and *Jupiter's* Diſtance from him to be about *five*, (conſidered with Reſpect to that of the Earth,) the Queſtion is to know how much the Sun's attractive Force will be diminiſhed at the Diſtance of *Jupiter*?

Give me a little Time to conſider, anſwered ſhe with ſome Impatience, for the Solution of a Problem is no trifling Affair. You have informed me that the attractive Force is ſo much leſs, as the Square of that Number which expreſſes the Diſtance is greater. The Square of one which is the Earth's Diſtance from the Sun, is *one*. And at the diſtance *one*, anſwered I, the Force is ſuppoſed to be *one*, and the Queſtion you are to reſolve is, How much that Force will be diminiſhed at the Diſtance of *Jupiter* from the Sun which is *five*. The Square of *five*, anſwered ſhe with great Quickneſs, is *twenty five*. If the attractive Force muſt be ſo much leſs as this Square is greater, it follows that in *Jupiter* it is twenty five times leſs than in the Earth. Is not this the Solution of your Problem? and may not I, like *Ar-*

chimedes,

chimedes, run crying about, *I have found it, I have found it?*

Yes certainly, anſwered I, but not in the ſame Circumſtance as he did, when his Impatience was ſo great as to make him run precipitately out of the Bath. The Mathematicians ought rather to act as *Pythagoras* did upon the Diſcovery of a certain Truth, and ſacrifice a Hecatomb to ſolemnize this Day which gives them Liberty to imbelliſh and brighten their gloomy Catalogue by your Name.

The Law that the attractive Force obſerves of growing weaker at various Diſtances from the Sun, is the very ſame to which all other Qualities that flow from Bodies, are ſubject; as Smell, Sound, Heat, and, which moſt nearly concerns us, Light. Thus when you believe yourſelf to have ſolved only one Problem, you have in reality ſolved two. Is then, replied ſhe, the Light of the Sun as well as his Attraction twenty five times leſs in *Jupiter* than with us? The very ſame Number, anſwered I, ſerves equally for both. After the ſame Manner

Manner you will find that the Attraction, the Light and Heat of the Sun, muſt be ninety times leſs in *Saturn* than with us. The Twilight of our fartheſt *Laplanders* would be there the fineſt Summer Days, and in the moſt raging Dog-ſtar of that Planet our Seas hardened with perpetual Ice, inſtead of ſwift ſailing Veſſels, would groan under the Weight of heavy Chariots; whereas in *Mercury* they would even in the Depth of Winter be diſſipated into thin Vapors (occaſioned by his extreme Proximity to the Sun) and would thus leave their Bottom dry, and preſent to Pilots a horrid Gulf, a dreadful View of the Terrors of the Deep; and to Naturaliſts a beautiful Scene that would furniſh them Materials to enrich their Muſæums.

You ſee, anſwered ſhe ſmiling, how many fine Diſcoveries I have made without perceiving any thing of it. It is however true, that great Affairs are generally brought to paſs we know not how, and we are at laſt amazed to find them effected.

In human Affairs, anſwered I, it is aſcribed

aſcribed to their good Fortune, if the *Cæſars* and *Alexanders* after propoſing only one End, acquire another which they never dream'd on. It often happens, that thoſe very Perſons who are called fortunate gain that Name by ſome Events very different from what they intended. The Inventer of Gunpowder, 'tis probable, propoſed a quite different End to his Studies than the Diſcovery of a Secret to deſtroy Mankind with the greater Facility; and that Perſon who found a new World ſought nothing but a more expeditious Way to the richeſt Part of the old.

On the other Hand, in true Natural Philoſophy and Geometry, the *Cæſars* and *Alexanders* are more common. It is very ſeldom that we find only what we ſought. The Diſcovery of one Truth frequently produces many others which appear in Spite, as it were, of thoſe who ſeemed to diſregard them. Any one who carefully ſeeks that Law by which the attractive Force ought to act at various Diſtances, will at the ſame Time diſcover that univerſal Law by which

which all the Qualities which flow from Bodies are governed. Natural Philosophy afterwards illustrates this general Truth with peculiar Experiments, and in some measure translates the abstruse Hieroglyphics of the learned Tongue into vulgar Language. That Decrease of the attractive Force which immediately concerns Light, is demonstrated by a very easy Experiment, which we may try this Evening, if you are not already sufficiently tired with Philosophy and Experiments.

Suppose one single Candle to be placed in a Room, and recede from it to such a Distance as not to be able to distinguish the Characters of a Book or a Letter, unless perhaps it were a Billet-doux, which may be read at any Distance.

Place yourself afterwards at a Distance twice as far from the Candle as you were at first. In this Situation the Force of the Light must be, according to the established Law, four times less than it was at the first Distance. The Letter then cannot be read with the ſame Diſtinctneſs as it was at firſt, unleſs the Light be *quadrupled*: That is, the Law requires that in the Proportion as the Light grows weaker, the Square of the Diſtance muſt increaſe. And this proves the Experiment to be true; for the Letter at the ſecond Diſtance is then only read with the ſame Diſtinctneſs as at the firſt, when three more Candles are added to the ſingle one, or, in other Words, when the Light is *quadrupled*.

Conſidering how very eaſily People are apt to forget thoſe Objects in their Abſence which made the greateſt Impreſſions upon their Mind when preſent, I cannot help thinking, ſaid the Marchioneſs, that this Proportion in the Squares of the Diſtances of Places, or rather of Times, is obſerved even in Love. Thus after eight Days Abſence Love becomes ſixty four times leſs than it was the firſt Day, and according to this Proportion it muſt ſoon be entirely obliterated; I fancy there will be found, eſpecially in the preſent Age, very few Experiments to the contrary. I believe, ſaid I, that both Sexes are included in this Theorem,

Theorem, which ſeems rather to follow the Cubes of the Times, which is certainly more convenient, and requires only four Days for an intire Oblivion. But, in general, I believe we may without Scruple eſtabliſh the Proportion of the Squares, for eight Days are commonly enough to cure the moſt vehement Paſſion. You alone have Power to reverſe this Theorem, and make the Remembrance of you, and with that a Deſire of ſeeing you, inſtead of diminiſhing, increaſe according to the Squares, or rather the Cubes of the Times. No! no! ſaid the Marchioneſs, Gallantry muſt never deſtroy a Theorem. I am willing to enter into the general Rule, and ſhall think myſelf exceedingly happy if I have been able to eſtabliſh any thing fixed and conſtant, in an Affair ſo inconſiſtent and wavering as Love. If Geometry, anſwered I, was permitted to get ſome Footing there, it would in a little Time produce Wonders. The Concluſions would be the moſt ready and elegant imaginable.

But to be ſerious, ſaid ſhe: Our Conclufion in Natural Philofophy was, That the attractive Force of the Sun diminifhes in Proportion as the Squares of the Diftances increafe. I fuppofe the attractive Force of the Planets will follow the fame Proportion with Regard to their Satellites. The Satellites, anfwered I, which turn about any Planet, obferve the fame Relation between the Diftances and the Times of their Revolutions, as the Planets themfelves do that turn about the Sun. This is evident in *Jupiter* and *Saturn*, who have more than one Satellite, and confequently the Law of their attractive Force will be the fame as that of the Sun.

In the Earth, who has only one fingle Satellite to her Share, this is not altogether fo evident. But what Reafon is there why it fhould not be the fame in one as in the other?

If we had another Satellite revolving about our Earth at a Diftance different from that of the Moon, it would difcover whether the attractive Force of the Earth obferves the fame Law as that of the Sun *Jupiter* and *Saturn*. This

Defect

Defect however is supplied by the Bodies which we see every Day fall upon the Surface of the Earth; for we are to believe that the Force which would make the Moon fall if she lost her Motion from West to East, is the very same that makes Bodies here below fall upon the Surface of the Earth when they are left to themselves: For since it is demonstrated that the Earth has an attractive Force, it is evident we must in this Force seek the Cause of Gravity, another Phænomenon, which the Vortices have been as unsuccessful in the Explication of, as in that of the planetary Motions.

If we could raise Bodies from the Earth to very considerable Distances (compared with that at which we stand from the Center which is very great,) we should see the Force of Gravity prodigiously diminished in them. A Man of War of a hundred Guns, for whose Formation a whole Forest was cut down, and a whole Mine exhausted, would be overset by the slightest Breeze of a *Zephyr*. The famous *Stone-Henge* upon *Salisbury* Plain, the fruitful Source of Fables both to the Learned and Ignorant, those *Colossian* Heaps which are held together by the Force of Gravity, would be no more than Houses built of Card. The Velocity in the Fall of heavy Bodies would be considerably retarded. Bombs, those artificial Thunders, would not be more terrible than so many Flakes of Snow. But these Experiments are impracticable; one of the greatest Distances we can attain is *Pike Teneriff*, which is only about three Miles perpendicularly high. Besides the Air would be too thin for Respiration, and the Cold, which must be exceedingly sharp at a greater Height, would render any Experiment fatal to the Philosopher who had the Courage to undertake it.

Nature, replied the Marchioness, has in this Case denied us the Means of being compleat *Newtonians*. She has here confined us within the Bounds of Probability. If the attractive Force observes a certain Law in the Sun, *Jupiter* and *Saturn*, why should not the same Force

observe

observe it here on our Earth? In this Point, answered I, we have no Reason to complain; we have no Need of higher Mountains, and a different Constitution of Air, in the present Case. All these Things, and the Defect of another Moon, are, as I before observed, supplied by the Bodies which fall upon the Surface of the Earth. We may compare these Bodies to the Moon herself; and thus instead of Probability we shall have Evidence, and be even in this Point good *Newtonians*.

It has been deduced from Observation, that if the Moon should lose her Motion, and fall towards the Earth, that Force which would set her a falling would be three thousand six hundred times less than the Force which makes Bodies fall upon the Surface of the Earth. You see how well this agrees with our Principle. The Moon is distant from the Center of the Earth (where the attractive Force chiefly resides) sixty times as far as these Bodies: The Square of sixty is 3600; The Attraction then of the Earth to the Moon is diminished in the same Proportion as the Square of the Distance is increased; and this is exactly agreeable to the established Law in *Jupiter*, *Saturn*, and the *Sun*.

If the Moon should happen to fall upon the Earth, replied the Marchioness, it would present a fine and agreeable Sight to the *Newtonians*: They would certainly have neither Curiosity, Eyes, nor Calculations for any thing else. This might very easily happen, answered I, if every thing was Body, as the *Cartesians* affirm; and those ancient *Gauls*, who were apprehensive the Heavens might one Day or other fall upon their Heads, would have some Reason to fear it in the System of their own *Des Cartes:* For it has been demonstrated that if this Planet was to move in a Place absolutely filled with Matter, without the least empty Space (let this Matter be supposed ever so subtile, fluid and æthereal) her Motion from West to East would be so retarded that it would soon grow weaker, and at length totally fail. And thus yielding to the Force of Gravity she would fall precipitately from

Heaven

Heaven to Earth, and we should no more behold her that *triform* Goddess we before admired, but a Stranger banished from the most shining of her three Kingdoms, and no longer the Ornament of Heaven amidst the friendly Silence of the Night.

The other Planets would undergo the same Fate if they moved in a Plenum. These would all, some sooner and others later, fall into the Sun, and supply that immense Volcano with a greater Quantity of Matter. He would then reign the Sovereign of a depopulated Empire: His animating Light would shine in vain: Not a single Planet would be left to partake his pleasing Influence, nor receive from him the Seasons and the Day; for both the Comets and we with our Moon should be stifled in him, if we met with any Obstacle in our æthereal Road. This would be a new Punishment to an Age fruitful of Crimes, in the System of that *English* Writer (*)

I 5 who

(*) Mr. *Swinden* in his Treatise *of the Nature and Place of Hell.*

who makes the glorious Body of the Sun the Mansion of Grief, and the Seat of eternal Despair.

I assure you, for my part, I should be one of the first, continued I, who would run to see the Moon fall upon the Earth. What an agreeable Spectacle would it be to see, in Proportion as she approached to us, that Face, that Mouth and Nose, which we discover in her rather by our Imagination than our Eyes, gradually transformed into great Mountains, Vallies, Plains and the like, which must certainly fill the Vulgar with great Astonishment: Nay even Philosophers themselves, who can never sufficiently master those two great Enemies of Reason, Fancy and Prejudice, could not help looking on this Phænomenon without some Degree of Surprize. As she approached still nearer, said the Marchioness, should not we descry the Sighs of Lovers, Dedications to Princes, Courtiers Promises, Vials filled with the Judgment of our Sages, and all the other lost Things which *Ariosto* places there? You have not

not read the Plurality of Worlds, anſwered I, and therefore are not capable of ſeeing the greateſt Curioſities in that Planet; ſince you are not yet acquainted with the Force of a *Why not*, which peoples the whole Univerſe.

But one Thing which I ſhould take great Pleaſure in obſerving, if the Moon ſhould really happen to fall, is, what Treatment the Earth would give the Moon in going to receive her.

What, replied the Marchioneſs, is it a Point of Ceremony eſtabliſhed among the Planets, that if a Satellite ſhould fall upon its Primary, the latter muſt go meet it and ſhorten its Way? This Ceremony, anſwered I, is founded upon mutual and reciprocal Attraction. If the Earth attracts the Moon, why ſhould not the Moon attract the Earth? The Attraction which the Earth exerciſes upon the Moon is lodged in that Matter of which the Earth is compoſed, why then ſhould not the Matter of which the Moon is compoſed exerciſe its attractive Force upon the Earth, ſince all Matter is entirely the ſame, and only

only differently modified in different Bodies? Besides *Action*, as the Philosophers express it, *is always equal to Reaction.* You cannot press this Table with your Finger, but it will be equally re-pressed by the Table. Thus if two little Gondolas made of Cork (in one of which is placed a Loadstone, and in the other a Piece of Iron) are set a floating upon the Water near each other, the Loadstone will run as fast towards the Iron as the Iron does towards the Loadstone; and if either of them be hindered, that left at Liberty will spring towards the other, which could not happen unless the Iron attracted the Loadstone as much as the Loadstone itself does the Iron, or, in short, unless their Attraction were reciprocal.

I perceive, said the Marchioness, what will be the Conclusion of all this. The Sun attracts the Planets, and consequently the Planets attract the Sun: The Secondaries attract each other, are all attracted by the Sun, and all attract him. Does not this Multiplicity, this

Chaos

Chaos of Attractions perplex not only me but the Syſtem itſelf too? No, Madam, anſwered I, it happens in this juſt as in the new Geometry (of which I was ſpeaking to you the other Day) in which all thoſe innumerable Orders of infinitely ſmall Quantities, inſtead of perplexing, render it more ſubtile and perfect.

This mutual Attraction, diffuſed through the Univerſe and all its Parts, retains the wandring Planets in their Orbits, and connects all Bodies, the Earth, and us ourſelves, by ſtrong tho' inviſible Ties, and regulates and tempers every Motion in ſuch a Manner, that its Exiſtence and irreſiſtible Laws are every Inſtant apparent.

In thinking on this reciprocal Attraction, ſaid the Marchioneſs, ſomething comes into my Mind, which I dare not however propoſe as an Objection to a Syſtem which the Philoſophers themſelves cannot venture to oppoſe. It appears to me that if there really was ſuch a mutual Attraction, we muſt ſee the Effects of it in thoſe Bodies

Bodies which surround us, if not every Instant, at least very often, just as we discover from their Gravity the Effects of that general Attraction which the Earth exercises upon them.

When any little light Body, as a Feather for Instance, be placed near a Palace, a Hill, or any Thing whose Attraction is very strong, why do not we see it presently obey the Force which attracts it, and move, as it should do, towards the Palace or Hill? When our Mind is possessed by a very strong Passion, answered I, what is the Reason we do not feel the weaker, unless it be that the strong Passion attracts the whole Soul, so as not to suffer the weaker to make any Impression upon it, and thus we become insensible to all the rest which are not in themselves either light or weak?

The furious Passion of *Phædra* for *Hippolytus* in *Racine* does not permit her to feel that strongest Passion in the Fair Sex, the Desire of Beauty. Her Ornaments and her whole Dress are in that Disorder which perhaps neither the Absence

nor

nor Death of her *Theseus* could ever have produced in them.

I comprehend you, replied the Marchioness, notwithstanding your parabolical Method of explaining this Point. The very great Attraction which Bodies feel from the Earth, if I may use the Expression, render them insensible to that of the other Bodies which surround them. Bodies, answered I, attract only in Proportion to the Quantity of Matter they contain. I make no Scruple of using mathematical Terms to you, for to use any other would be an Affront to a Person who has given the Solution of a Problem.

Thus a Ball of Gold, besides many other Advantages, has a greater attractive Power than that of Wood, because it has a greater Weight; and if the first be a hundred times heavier than the last, that is, if it contains a hundred times greater Quantity of Matter, it will have its attractive Power a hundred times stronger.

Now the Attraction of this great Ball upon which we stand is diffused on all

all Sides, and draws every Thing to it with an immense Force, and by that Means hinders us from perceiving the Effects of that particular Force, which the little Balls by which we are surrounded exercise upon each other.

A Globe of the same Density with the Earth, and of a Foot Diameter, attracts any little Body placed near its Superficies, twenty Million times less than the Earth does. The Attraction of the highest Mountains as that of *Pike Teneriff*, *Ararat*, or even the *Apennine*, notwithstanding the pompous Description made of it, is absolutely imperceptible.

But it is not so with the Effects of the Lunar Attraction upon this vast Collection of Waters that some Philosopher made the first Principle of Things, which by the easy Method of Navigation joins the most distant Countries, and transports to us from another World those Balms and Aromatics which season the *European* Entertainments. You seem, replied the Marchioness, to have a very lively

lively Senſe of our Obligations to the Ocean, and the Advantages we receive from it. But has not the Philoſopher amidſt theſe Entertainments forgot the Attraction of the Moon? The Ocean, anſwered I, every Day ſhews us the Effects of this Attraction, which extends its Empire throughout all Nature. The Ebbing and Flowing of the Sea, a Phænomenon, which, in the moſt poliſhed Age of *Greece*, *Alexander* the Great took as a Mark of the Divine Diſpleaſure, and with which the *Romans* in the Golden Age of *Julius Cæſar* were but very little acquainted, is only a Conſequence of that Attraction the Moon exerciſes upon the fluid and yielding Part of our Globe. *Chapelle* in his celebrated Voyage, that Model of polite and agreeable Wit, believed that no one but a Water-God could penetrate into its Cauſe.

This God relates to him, that when *Neptune* was made Governor of the Sea, the Rivers went to congratulate him. The *Garonne* upon this Occaſion retained ſomething of the haughty Temper of his Country, and his Compliments were not

ſo

so submissive as was necessary in addressing that Power who raises the Tempest by a single Nod, and with an *I will* —— silences them to a profound Calm.

The Punishment which this arrogant River received for his Crime, was to be repelled twice a Day back to his Source. All the Rivers which flow twice a Day into the Ocean undergo the same Fate. But why, answered the Marchioness, should the other Rivers who were not guilty of this Gascon Behaviour suffer the same Punishment as the *Garonne*? If it was permitted to make Objections to Superior Powers, I would humbly propose this to *Chapelle*'s Neptune.

You may make Objections equally strong, answered I, to all the human Systems that have been made to explain this Phænomenon. Some affirmed the Respiration of this vast Animal the Earth and the Sea to be the Reason of it, others a great Gulf in the Northern Ocean near *Norway*, which emits a vast Quantity of Water and afterwards swallows it up again; a most fatal Circumstance both for the Fishes and Philosophy

Philoſophy which have the Misfortune to be plunged in its Deeps. The ancient *Chineſe*, who ſuppoſed their little Country of four Leagues Extent, to be the Univerſe itſelf, aſſerted that two great Nations deſcended from a certain Princeſs, the one inhabiting the Mountains, and the other the Sea-ſhore, had frequent Wars with each other, and this was the Reaſon of the Flux and Reflux according as either of the Combatants was drove back towards the Mountains or the Sea.

Such perhaps was the Infancy of Philoſophy among all, even the moſt ſagacious People. The Explication of *Des Cartes* which was produced in a later Age of the World is ingenious enough to render it agreeable, but not accurate enough to be true. The ſame *Engliſh* Philoſopher who caſt an impenetrable Obſcurity over Viſion, by involving it in his contractile and expanſive Forces, has endeavoured to involve this Phænomenon alſo in the ſame unintelligible Terms. This gloomy Fancy diffuſed itſelf like an univerſal Contagion over

over the whole Face of Things, and infected the whole Syſtem of Natural Philoſophy.

According to his Opinion, the moſt ſimple and evident Method of explaining the Tides, is by aſcribing their Cauſe to the contractive Forces of the Earth and Moon, by which the one raiſes and the other depreſſes the Water. To theſe he unites the expanſive Force of the Sun, which, tho' always contrary to the contractive, yet upon this Occaſion muſt act in Concert with that of the Moon. Theſe unintelligible Terms, which have not ſo much as the Faſhion to ſupport them, can imply nothing in the Author but a vehement and vain Deſire of giving his Name to a new Syſtem of Errors. Theſe Philoſophers, ſaid ſhe, appear to me the Prieſts of *Chapelle's* Divinity: Their Explications at once diſcover both the Temerity and Weakneſs of their Philoſophy. Our's, anſwered I, takes delight in Difficulties, and comes off in Triumph; amidſt the Thorns we are ſure at leaſt to meet with Roſes.

That

That Portion of the Water immediately under the Moon and nearest to her, must be more strongly attracted than the rest which she looks obliquely on, and which is at the greatest Distance from her. The Ocean then must flow together from all Parts, and be heaped into a Mountain of Waters whose Summit will be under the Moon herself.

The Earth itself is a little attracted by the Moon, but that Part of the Water which is directly opposite to the Part under the Moon is least attracted, because it is at the greatest Distance.

This Part then will be as it were forsaken by the Earth which a little follows the Attraction of the Moon, and will there form the Summit of another watery Mountain, and thus there will be two, the one totally opposite to the other.

The Ocean then must swell, and in some measure lengthen itself in that Part where the Moon is, and in the Part opposite to her, and thus from the Figure of an Apple be changed to that of of a Lemon, whoſe Extremities will always follow the Moon in her diurnal Courſe; ſo that the Water will be at one Time depreſſed, and at another raiſed, both in the ſame Place.

In every Part of the Ocean there will be two Tides, during the Time which the Moon employs in returning to the ſame Point of the Heavens. When ſhe is at the Meridian the Waters muſt be raiſed, and when ſhe ſets, depreſſed; another Elevation when ſhe is at the Meridian of the *Antipodes*, and another Depreſſion when ſhe riſes.

All this muſt unavoidably happen if the whole Earth was covered with deep Waters, and they immediately obeyed the attractive Force of the Moon. But becauſe there is ſome Time neceſſary for the accumulating the Waters, and their Courſe is interrupted by Shores, Straights, Iſlands, and the like, there are ſome Irregularities in the Tides.

Theſe Irregularities however are not ſo great, but twice in every twenty five Hours (which is nearly the Time that the Moon employs in her Return to the Me-

Meridian) we ſee the Veſſels laden with the Riches of the Univerſe go up with the Tide along the Silver Waves of the *Thames*, and twice deſcend with the Reflux to go in Queſt of new Treaſures. And this Advantage, which in the Syſtem of *Chapelle* was inflicted as a Puniſhment, all the Rivers which flow into the Ocean enjoy.

Have our *Mediteranean* Rivers, ſaid the Marchioneſs, ever offended the Moon, that they are not ſuffered to enjoy the ſame Advantage? Perhaps they have affronted her as the *Garonne* did *Neptune*.

The Straight, anſwered I, by which the *Mediteranean* has a Communication with the Ocean, is too narrow for ſo great a Sea, and is diſadvantageouſly ſituated, (ſince it looks towards the Weſt) to receive the great Flood of the Ocean that follows the Moon from Eaſt to Weſt.

On the other hand, the Tide which is formed in the *Mediteranean* itſelf is too much interrupted with Iſlands, Shores and Straights, for the Flux and

Reflux

Reflux to be very considerable. In the *Adriatic*, on the contrary, it is more sensible than in any other Place, because the Sea is very narrow, just as the Motion of a River is most apparent and seems most rapid when confined between the Arches of a Bridge. In our fine City founded by the Gods upon the Ocean, the Vicissitudes of the Flux and Reflux carry the fluctuating Gondolas from one Side to another, while the Gondolier sits at his Ease and singing to the agreeable Light of the Moon, teaches the Sea-nymphs the Flight of *Erminia*, or *Rinaldo*'s Love.

The Changes of the Tydes are still less perceptible in the *Baltic-Sea*, the *Mediterranean* of the North; for this Sea bordering upon the frozen Regions of the *Pole*, and very distant from the Course of the Moon, seems more adapted to Ice and Rocks than to Warmth and Attraction.

In the Shores of the southern and oriental Oceans, to *Japan* and *China*, the Tyde is very considerable by reason of the Extent of the Seas; and

in

in our Ocean its Effects are incredibly prodigious. There are Coasts near *Dunkirk*, where the Sea draws back for the Space of several Miles, and afterwards on a sudden returns and overflows the same Space again, alternately covering and disclosing those Sands so very suspicious to Sailors, not without sometimes disturbing the Ladies in that Country, who venture to walk upon the Margin of the Sea, whose very Shores are faithless and deceitful. These are a Sort of natural Sea Fights, where at some Parts in the Day two Armies may engage on dry Land, and at others, two Fleets, at least such as those of the Ancients were.

In some Rivers the Tide rises to more than fifty Foot high, especially if the Sun and Moon act in Conjunction to render the Flood considerable.

Tho' the Moon may be regarded as Empress of the Ocean, the Sun however has his Share in it. Notwithstanding he is at a greater Distance from the Earth than the Moon is, yet in Return he is so much greater, that it is not proper he ſhould remain idle, but lend his Part to the Production of the Tides. The reſt of the heavenly Bodies have no ſenſible Influence in this Caſe, the vaſt Diſtance they are ſeparated from us renders them too ſmall.

When the Moon is in her Quadratures the Tydes are leſs than at any other Times in the Month. The Reaſon of this is, becauſe the attractive Forces of the Sun and Moon croſſing each other, are as contrary as is poſſible to the Swelling of the Sea in the ſame Situation.

On the other Hand, when the Moon is new or full, ſhe is in the ſame direct Line with the Sun in reſpect to the Earth, their Forces are united, and then the Tides are higheſt.

It is to be obſerved however, that the Motion begun in the Waters and retained for ſome Time within them, muſt be ſome Days after the new or full Moon, before it produces the greateſt Raiſing of the Sea. So in Summer, the Heat of Mid-day that remains in the Air, being added to the following-ing Heat, leſs intenſe in itſelf, is the Reaſon why we have not ſo great need of the Aſſiſtance of the Fan to ſupply us with freſh Air at Noon itſelf, as we have ſome Hours after.

The greateſt of all the Tides happens at the new or full Moon of the Equinoxes; for beſides the Conjunction of the ſolar and lunar Force, the Waters in this Caſe acquire a greater Agitation; but becauſe the Sun (notwithſtanding our freezing) is nearer to the Earth in Winter than in Summer, theſe great Tides do not happen at the preciſe Time of the Equinoxes, but a little before the Vernal, and ſomething later than the Autumnal, that is, in the Month of *February* and *October*.

In *Mercury*, *Venus*, and *Mars* the Tides are governed by the Sun alone, tho' they muſt be almoſt inſenſible in *Mars*, becauſe that Planet is at ſo great a Diſtance from him. In *Jupiter* and *Saturn* the Diſtance from the Sun is ſo very great, that he can have abſolutely no Influence over the Tides. They will confound each other according

ing to the Caprice of the Satellites, the great Number of which will render them very irregular.

If we knew the Time of *Saturn*'s Rotation as we do that of *Jupiter*'s, and were as well acquainted with the Geography of both, and the Quantity of Matter contained in their Moons, as we are with their Diſtances and Revolutions, we might conjecture the Quantity and Period of their Tides, and ſend Tables of them to their Pilots. Thus are we again tranſported by Attraction into Heaven, to vaſt and remote Worlds where this powerful Quality holds its moſt conſpicuous and ſhining Seat.

By the Help of this, replied the Marchioneſs, we can travel thouſands of Miles in an Inſtant, and are well recompenſed by innumerable great and ſhining Truths. A *French* Author, I anſwered, a zealous Propagator of this Syſtem, like us tranſported by Attraction to theſe diſtant Worlds, thinks with great Probability, that the Moons of *Jupiter* and *Saturn* as well as ours had once been Comets, which paſſing near

enough

enough to theſe Planets to remain confined within the Sphere of their Attraction, were conſtrained to revolve round them, and thus degraded from the Rank of Primary to that of Secondary Planets.

Saturn has obtained ſo advantageous a Situation as to make him the moſt happy in the Number of his Conqueſts. For the ſame Reaſon he was able to acquire a fine Ring that incompaſſes his Body, and which was formerly a Comet that unhappily paſſed too near him.

This *Saturn*, replied the Marchioneſs, muſt be very terrible to the Comets that approach a little too cloſe to him. He muſt be the ſame to them as the *Cabo tormentoſo*, to which Avarice afterwards gave the Name of *Good Hope*, was to the *Portugueze*. It muſt, I fancy, have been a very agreeable Sight to ſee *Saturn* at once adorn and enrich himſelf with a ſplendid Ring, while the poor Comet was forced to purſue its Journey, ſpoiled of the Honour of its ſhining Train.

He robbed it of nothing, anſwered

I, but what it enjoyed at another's Expence, according to the Supposition of a certain *French* Author, who assures us that the Comet in crossing the Atmosphere of the Sun, had from thence stolen its Tail. But the *Newtonian* Opinion is, that the Tails of Comets are formed and composed of certain Vapours arising from the Comets themselves when they are near the Sun.

Is it not a very great Advantage, replied the Marchioness, to be possessed of a System that supplies even the Imagination with the most pleasing Amusement, by those strange and surprising Events which it renders possible? And all this, answered I, only by the Force that among us makes a Stone fall to the Earth. This Attraction, said she, appears to be the same in the Hand of Nature, as the Subject of a Composition in that of a skilful Musician. Be it never so simple, yet when he undertakes it he will diversify it a thousand Ways, and make it appear every Moment new; in short, he will find enough

in

in it to form the moſt harmonious Concert in the World.

Nature, continued I, wants no other Subject at once to regulate and vary thoſe innumerable and vaſt planetary Syſtems, which probably revolve round the fixed Stars, thoſe luminous and attractive Suns that chear the Night, and which we debaſe by giving them the Names of our miſerable Heroes. But why ſhould theſe Heroes, ſaid the Marchioneſs, remain unmoved and fixt? If they have a mutual Attraction, how comes it to paſs that they do not approach each other and run all together? You have, perhaps, ſome other Parable ready which only waited till I ſhould propoſe a Difficulty. No Madam, anſwered I, unleſs you take it for a Parable when I tell you that this would exactly happen, if the Number of thoſe Suns was not infinite. Thoſe which are upon the Superficies of this immenſe Sphere of Suns would be united to thoſe next them, becauſe they would not have any thing to attract them a contrary Way, and by that Means keep them in their Orbits. And thus theſe ſucceſſively running into thoſe next them, and theſe laſt into others, they would be all heaped together. By this Means in a little Time there would be in the whole Univerſe only one Sun of an enormous Size.

But what is the Number of theſe Suns? What are the Limits of their Sphere? Is not the Center of it throughout, and the Circumference in no Place? The Difficulty you have moved would be alone ſufficient to induce us to multiply the Stars *ad infinitum*, even if we had not a thouſand Reaſons beſides.

I am quite loſt, replied the Marchioneſs, in this Infinity of Suns and planetary Worlds; pray let us return to our own. We are poſſeſſed of a Syſtem capable of diverſifying it to Infinity, if we were ſo fond of Infinity as to deſire it. And a Syſtem, anſwered I, which predicts and gives a Reaſon for the very ſmalleſt Irregularities that can happen. After Attraction and its Laws were eſtabliſhed, how ſublime a Geometry was requiſite to find out what Path the Planets muſt keep in the Spaces

ces of Heaven, and how much more sublime still to foresee exactly how much they would deviate from that Path in the Constitution of the present System? The Vastness of the Object renders general Rules difficult, and the Niceness of the Variations renders the Exceptions still more difficult.

The Sun who was esteemed immoveable in the Center of the System, and imagined himself exempt from any Irregularity, is found however to be subject to it; for the Attraction between Bodies is always mutual, and every Cause must have a correspondent Effect proportioned to its Activity. As the Planets and Sun reciprocally attract each other, he must be sensible of their Force; so that to speak with the utmost Rigour, he continually changes *his*, as they vary *their* Situation with Respect to him. After all our Speculations then, replied the Marchioness, to prove the Immoveability of the Sun, we are at last reduced to make him move again. Had it not been better, continued she with a certain malicious Smile, to adhere to the common Opinion without giving ourſelves all this Trouble? Do not you act like thoſe Perſons who after employing their Reaſon to diveſt themſelves of popular Prejudices, are afterwards obliged to have Recourſe to the ſame Reaſon to reſume them, if they have an Inclination to live and converſe with their fellow Mortals?

Our Caſe, anſwered I, is extremely different. The Queſtion then was to make the Sun revolve about the Earth with ſuch a Motion as to run a Million and a Half of Miles in one Day. But at preſent the Earth herſelf continues to revolve about the Sun, and he has no other Employment than to approach or recede a little ſometimes towards one and ſometimes towards another Side of the common Center of the whole Syſtem. This Motion is inſenſible in Aſtronomy, and is in Fact only a mathematical Subtlety with which I thought myſelf obliged to make you acquainted. If the Planets were all on one Side, you are ſenſible that their united Forces muſt act upon him with the greateſt poſſible Strength, in order to draw him back to them-

ſelves

ſelves and make him recede from the Center of the Syſtem: They would not however attract him, conſidering the Enormity of his Bulk, any more than one of his Diameters. I am very willingly convinced of my Error, ſaid ſhe. The Sun, who notwithſtanding his vaſt Size is ſubject to the general Force of Gravity, may ſerve for an Example to great Kings, whom neither the Extent of their Fortune, nor the Superiority of their Station can ever exempt from an Obſervation of the univerſal Laws of Humanity.

Our Moon, continued I, is at preſent ſubjected by Attraction to the minuteſt and moſt exact Calculations of Aſtronomers. Her very Irregularities, her Caprices are reduced to certain and conſtant Rules. Comets, thoſe Enemies of Syſtems who made ſtill greater Reſiſtence to the Power of Numbers than the Moon herſelf, are at length obliged to revolve about the Sun. And tho' their Orbits are much more oblong than thoſe of the Planets, yet they obſerve exactly the ſame Laws.

By

By Obſervations made upon their Appearances Philoſophers have aſſigned what Orbits the Comets muſt run in this Syſtem, and theſe in Fact are the Orbits which they really have run, almoſt with the ſame Exactneſs as the other Planets, notwithſtanding the imperfect Obſervations left us by the Ancients concerning Comets, the Moderns have ventured to predict the Return of ſome of them, in the ſame Manner as they do Eclipſes. And indeed what is there which this Syſtem might not authoriſe? A *Titian* could eaſily judge of a Picture from a rough Draught.

The Prophecy of that Ancient is now fully accompliſhed, who even in his Time foreſaw that Poſterity would calculate the Periods and predict the Returns of theſe Bodies, theſe eternal Monuments of the Ignorance and Weakneſs of human Nature.

It is expected that the Comets which appeared in 1658 will return twenty three Years hence, and I hope we may flatter ourſelves we ſhall obſerve it together, you ſtill young, and I not very old.

old. You ſhall be the *Urania* to give a right Direction to my Teleſcope. What a Viciſſitude of Things, replied the Marchioneſs, is there in this Syſtem! I am metamorphoſed into a *Urania*, and ſuppoſed to be young at a Time when it becomes unpolite to talk about Years, and the Non-Appearance of a Comet rendered more fatal than its Appearance! It will appear too ſoon, anſwered I, to put us in Remembrance of our paſt Time, and our Attraction. In this Caſe, replied ſhe, we may expreſs ourſelves contrary to the common Saying,

'Tis Expectation makes a Bleſſing dear.

'Tis at preſent indeed a great Happineſs to be an Aſtronomer. They at leaſt expect nothing in vain, and how great a Pleaſure do they owe to this Syſtem, which gives them a full Power over every Thing in that Heaven which is the Object of their Projects and Deſires?

Nothing, anſwered I, was a greater Curioſity

Curiosity to Astronomers, or more glorious for the *Newtonian* System, than the Conjunction of *Jupiter* and *Saturn* which happened in the Beginning of the present Age, an Age so fertile in the most surprizing Events. These two great Planets were to approach each other, which the vast Extent of their Orbits, and the Time employed in describing those Orbits, had not very often suffered them to do.

If it could ever be hoped to see the Effects of this mutual Attraction in the Disturbance and Alterations in the Motions of the Planets, it was upon this Occasion when the two most powerful in the whole Solar System approached each other, at a Distance however of three hundred and fifty Million of Miles. This was an Observation in *great*, as decisive for the *Newtonian* celestial System as the Experiments of refracting the coloured Rays with a second Prism, in order to prove whether Colour was a Modification of Light or no, was in *little*. The Curiosity in this Affair was so much the greater, because the *New-*

tonian

tonian Syſtem was then in its Infancy and Time which gives Strength to Truth, and in which Error vaniſhes away, had not yet decided any thing to the World in its Favour.

The Diſturbance which *Jupiter* the greateſt of all the Planets occaſioned in the Motions of *Saturn*, and that which this Planet reciprocally exerciſed upon the Satellites of *Jupiter*, were ſo conſiderable that they could not eſcape the Obſervations and Teſtimony of Aſtronomers, even thoſe who were the leaſt inclined to adopt the Syſtem, whom a Difference of Opinion from the Wagers held againſt it, might eaſily induce to regard this Phænomenon in a very ſuperficial Manner. And Sir *Iſaac Newton* had the Pleaſure of extorting from his very Enemies ſo ſtrong and ſolemn a Confirmation of his Syſtem. What are the Triumphs of the *Cæſars* and *Alexanders* (thoſe miſerable Conquerors who overturned two Particles of this Globe) when compared to the philoſophical Triumph of him who firſt diſcovered the vaſt Extent of the Univerſe?

Aſtronomy, ſaid the Marchioneſs, has

has by this Triumph amply rewarded Sir *Iſaac Newton* for defending it ſo well in the Affair of total Eclipſes. This mutual Aſſiſtance, this Commerce, if I may uſe the Expreſſion, of Truth, muſt certainly be a very great Honour to the Sciences. This Commerce, anſwered I, was never more evidently ſeen than in Attraction. We may affirm that every Science with a Sort of Emulation contributes to confirm this Truth, juſt as the whole World anciently did to the raiſing the *Roman* Empire.

Tho' I told you that the Effects of Attraction are more remarkable in the Heavens than any where elſe, yet it is alſo very evident in all Natural Philoſophy, Hydroſtatics, Chemiſtry, and Anatomy itſelf. Mr. *Muſcembrook* (who even in Philoſophy preſents the Character of a true Republican) confeſſes with that Freedom that becomes a Member of the *Belgic* State, that for the Space of many Years ſpent in the greateſt Variety of Experiments, he has obſerved in all Bodies certain Motions and Effects which could not be explained

or

or underſtood by Means of the external Preſſure of any ambient Fluid: But that Nature proclaims aloud a Law infuſed in Bodies by which they are attracted, without a Dependance upon Impulſion. Chemical Fermentations, the Hardneſs of Bodies, the round Figure of Drops of Water, and of the Earth itſelf, the Separation of the Juices in the human Body, the Suction of Water by Spunges, its Aſcent in thoſe Tubes which from their extreme Smallneſs are called *capillary*, and a thouſand other Things are inconteſtable Arguments for this Attraction. I believe that after ſo many repeated Proofs you will permit me to introduce it triumphantly into Optics, in order to explain the Effects which depend on this mutual Attraction betwixt Light and Bodies. It would be very extraordinary, ſaid ſhe, if I ſhould refuſe to admit the mutual Attraction of Light and Bodies, after I have ſeen the *Sun* and *Saturn* attract each other at ſo enormous a Diſtance.

Not to ſay any thing more of Diffraction, anſwered I, is not Refraction an an Effect of this attractive Power? Does it not arise from hence, that the Mediums through which the Light passes are indued with this Force in a greater or less Degree, according to the greater or less Density of the Medium? Otherwise the immense Force of the Earth which attracts every Thing to herself, would render it impossible for any Prism, if it were as big as Pike *Teneriff*, to attract the smallest Ray of Light.

While the Light passes through the same Medium because it is equally attracted on all Sides, it will not decline to any, but move forward according to that Direction it received from the Sun or any other luminous Body: If in its Way it meets with another Medium of a greater Force (such as Glass for Example compared to Air) must it not decline towards this Medium and immerse into it, approaching more or less to a Perpendicular as the Attraction of the new Medium is more or less powerful?

In going out of Glass into Air, the Light

Light is again attracted by the Air and the Glaſs; but becauſe the Force of the Glaſs is greater than that of the Air, the Light will remain behind the Surface of the Glaſs from whence it goes out, or behind that of the Air into which it enters, and which immediately touches the Glaſs itſelf.

Thus you ſee how eaſily by the Help of Attraction is explained a Phænomenon, which *Des Cartes* could not account for, unleſs by ſuppoſing that Light could with greater Facility paſs through denſe than rare Mediums; which is in other Words ſaying, that what makes the greateſt Reſiſtance to all other Bodies, muſt by ſome other Privilege of which I am ignorant, make the leaſt Reſiſtance to this. It is ſurpriſing to ſee how all that Experiments have diſcovered to happen in Refractions, are geometrically deduced from this Explication of the *Newtonian* Philoſophy.

To me, replied the Marchioneſs, who cannot enter into the Sanctuary of the Mathematics, it ſeems a ſufficient Proof that

that as the attractive Force is greater in Proportion as the Denſity of the Medium is ſo, the Refraction muſt in that Caſe be proportionably greater.

The *Dutch*, anſwered I, have found it to be much greater in *Nova Zembla* than here among us. The Air is extremely cold, and conſequently denſe in this Country, the Habitation of white Bears, and ſome *Europeans*, the miſerable Victims of the Avarice or Curioſity of their Species.

By the Help of this very great Refraction they had the Pleaſure of ſeeing the Sun after his long Abſence many Days before the Science of Coſmography had permitted him to appear, and the Denſity of the Air, which generally oppreſſes and damps the Spirits, ſerved in this Retreat of Miſery and Darkneſs, to revive their Imagination by an unexpectedly early Light.

We may at preſent hope for more exact Obſervations upon the Denſity of the Air and the Refractions of this Climate, which have never yet been examined by philoſophical Eyes. A learned Com-

Company is now ſetting Sail from *France* to the *Bothnic* Gulf, and another to *Peru*, in order by their united Obſervations to determine if poſſible the true Figure of the Earth, and animated by the Love of Science, have the Reſolution to change the Gardens and the delightful Seats of Pleaſure in their own Country for the frozen Rocks and Deſarts of *Lapland*.

In *North America* the Colds are incomparably more ſharp than in *Europe* at the ſame Diſtance from the Pole. There are in thoſe Seas Mountains of Ice of the ſame Date perhaps as the World, among which are ſometimes found Ships at full Sail as motionleſs as upon dry Land.

Doctor *Halley*, whom the *Engliſh* Nation regards with the higheſt Reſpect as the Friend and Companion of the great Sir *Iſaac Newton*, and whoſe Thoughts are employed on no Objects that are little or trifling, believes that theſe Countries were once perhaps nearer the Pole than they at preſent are, that a Comet by giving a Shock to the Earth

altered

altered their Situation and by this Means ſet them at a greater Diſtance. But that notwithſtanding this the great Magazine of Ice formed before this terrible Shock ſtill remains, nor has the Heat of following Ages ever been able to melt it. Hence proceed the ſharp Colds and a ſtronger Refraction cauſed by them.

Certain *Engliſh* Sailors who above a Century ago endeavoured without Succeſs, to find in *North America* a Paſſage to the Southern Sea, were obliged to ſpend the Winter in an Iſland very little more North than *London*. Every Thing there was transformed to Ice, the Houſe they had built, the Sea, the Ship, and even themſelves.

They were obliged to cut the moſt ſpirituous Wine with a Hatchet, and the Refraction was ſo ſtrong that they obſerved the riſing Moon of an oval Figure extremely long, and the Sun when at the Horizon to be twice as big in Breadth as in Length. The Air was ſometimes ſo very clear in the Depth of that ſevere Winter, that they diſco-vered

vered more Stars by two Thirds than are uſually ſeen, and the milky Way appeared evidently to the naked Eye a Collection of Stars. Thus in theſe Countries there would have been no Need of a *Democritus* to conjecture it among the Dreams of the ancient Philoſophy, nor a *Galileo* to verify it by the Aſſiſtance of the Teleſcope.

From a great Number of Experiments made in *England* it evidently appears, that the refractive Power of the Air increaſes in Proportion to its Denſity, which is true likewiſe in other Mediums which refract the Light, but however with ſome Exceptions. Air, Water and Glaſs ſenſibly obſerve this Proportion. But oleaginous and ſulphureous Liquors, and which conſequently are combuſtible, have a greater Refraction than Liquors of another Nature even if they are more denſe. Oyl which is leſs denſe than Water, as appears by its ſwimming upon it, has however a great Force in refracting the Light.

Alas! interrupted the Marchioneſs, I am a great Enemy to Exceptions, and

I have a most mortal Aversion to the *but* in Conversation. Every one who takes it into his Head to rail against our Sex before our very Face, will doubtless except, with a constrained *but*, her who has the Misfortune to be present. Satire so agreeable to the Malignity of our Mind, becomes cold with these Exceptions, our Self-love is not sufficiently flattered, and Truth loses too much when it becomes less general.

Exceptions of this Sort, answered I, are properly only new Truths which arise from the Discovery of many Causes, which joined together generally concur to produce a certain Effect. This greater Refraction in a less Density of Medium arises from another particular Correspondence between these Liquors and Light. It acts upon them more than upon any other Sort, by agitating, warming, and inflaming them more easily. It is just then, on the other Hand, that these in Return should act more upon the Light than other Mediums do, by breaking and refracting it in a greater Degree.

May

May we not conclude from hence that this Force resides chiefly in the sulphureous Parts of Bodies? For this Reason boiling Water, in which these Parts are more disengaged, has a greater attractive Force than cold Water.

In general, Warmth and Rubbing augment the attractive Force which is in Bodies, or make it appear it in a particular Manner. Amber, all Sorts of pellucid Gems, Glass, Hair, and many other Things when they are rubbed, discover the Force called *Electrical*, and which is communicated to other Bodies, carried to incredible Distances, and whose Effects are surprizing beyond all Belief.

If a Tube of Glass be rubbed till it gets hot, it will attract light Bodies as Leaves of Gold or Cotton, and afterwards drive them at a Distance. It will raise a Sort of Tempest in a Heap of little Pieces of burnt Paper by attracting and then tumultuously repelling them from itself. In short, this Force is a Species of magic Wand, that communicates and awakens a

Power in Bodies, which had before lain dormant and inactive.

A Ball of Ivory faſtened to a Cord of nine hundred or a thouſand Foot long acquires the ſame Power of Attraction and Repulſion, if the electrical Tube be applied to the other End of the Cord a thouſand Foot diſtant. You had very great Reaſon, replied the Marchioneſs, to call this Tube a Sort of magic Wand, for it really produces incomprehenſible Effects. At leaſt, it is a Myſtery to me that it ſhould with ſuch Rapidity draw the little Bodies to itſelf, and afterwards with a Sort of Diſdain remove and drive them away.

Obſervation, anſwered I, which has hitherto been our Guide and Clue in the intricate Labyrinth of Natural Philoſophy, will continue to give us the ſame Aſſiſtance in that little Way we have yet to go. It has conducted us to the Diſcovery of new Properties in Light and Colours, which have opened a new Scene of Optics to Philoſophy. It has conducted us to the Diſcovery of Attraction in the moſt ſecret Retreats of of Bodies; which is likewise a new and surprizing Quality of Matter, by which all Natural Philosophy is changed and renewed; and now this faithful Guide leads us to *Repulsion*, whose Effects in Nature are no less considerable and surprizing.

Are we not to impute it to this Force, that Flies are able to walk upon the Water without wetting their Legs, and that the Particles, which fly off from Bodies by Means of Heat or Fermentation, are set at so great a Distance from each other as to possess an infinitely greater Space than they did at first?

The Air after being compressed may be dilated to such a Degree as to possess a Space more than eight hundred twenty six thousand times greater than it did when compressed, and this without being heated, which would dilate it still more. That you may understand this Force has no less Influence in Heaven than Earth, the famous Comet of 1682 approached so close to the Sun that it was heated two thousand times more than a red hot Iron. The Vapours arising from it, and cast at a Distance from each other by the repulsive Force, adorned it with so formidable a Tail that it took up in Heaven the Length of eighty Million *English* Miles. It would have been very bad for us to have been near, and involved in it, for instead of gaining a Ring or another Moon, we should have been calcined and burnt to Ashes like a little Stone in the Focus of a burning Glass.

Some Persons so taken up with the Phantoms of the uncertain *Future*, as not to see the Fugitive *Present*, expect that one Day some Comet will cause the universal Conflagration of this Globe. Comets have perhaps anciently produced a Deluge; have struck against the Earth and overset every Thing in it, and who knows but one Time or other they may bring a Conflagration upon it, after which laying aside its old Spoils like the Snake, it may again grow young and be renewed, and our great Theatre change both its Scenes and Actors.

The present, replied she, is so various and agreeable as it now stands, that

I am greatly deceived if it may not divert us as yet a long Time without any Change.

But perhaps it is to these Comets that we are obliged for one of the finest Changes, and what we every Day enjoy. They are perhaps the ingenious Mechanists that have rendered our Theatre capable of being turned round like that of *Curio*, so famous in Antiquity, where the *Roman* People, the Conqueror of the World, the Race of Heroes, and the Portion granted to Mankind by the immortal Gods, sat upon a frail Machine, in which they could not even applaud their public Shews without Danger. We at present perhaps owe to some Comet (without apprehending any calamitous Accident) the Rotation of our Earth, the perpetual and constant Succession of Light and Shadow; in short, the pleasing Variety of Day and Night. One of these perhaps by giving us a Shock has occasioned this Motion in us as well as the other Planets which are discovered to be indued with it.

Before this we had, like the cold Inhabitants of the Pole, ſix Months Day and ſix Months Night, but without gaining like them either a ſtrong Refraction or a long Twilight to anticipate and prolong our Day. A little Moon-light would from Time to Time have faintly illuminated that long and melancholy Darkneſs. What Optics, what Colours could we ever have had for ſix continued Months, unleſs the Comet with its Shock had lent us its Aſſiſtances. Since every Thing, replied the Marchioneſs, ſtands well at preſent, Heaven guard us for the future from the Proximity of any one of them, from the Shocks, the Conflagrations and the Deluge with which they menace us, and from that repulſive Force that renders them ſo very formidable. But are not theſe the Riddles as well as Terrors of Natural Philoſophy, that the ſame Bodies ſhould be both attracted and repelled?

I do not know, anſwered I after ſome Pauſe, whether I ought to introduce you any farther into the Sanctuary of the *Newtonian* Philoſophy. There are in in this certain Myſteries ſtill deeper and more ſublime than thoſe to which you have already been admitted. You ſhould now invoke thoſe Spirits the firſt-born Sons of Light, the Guardians of thoſe ſecret Truths which they imparted to our Philoſopher, that they would ſuffer me to diſcover to you Things concealed from the Sight of Mortals, and deeply immerſed in a gloomy Miſt and the moſt profound Night. You muſt now entirely diveſt yourſelf of thoſe few Remains of Profaneneſs which may ſtill attend you. Tell me, Madam, what Courage do you feel for Truth? The ſame, anſwered ſhe, that a brave Soldier feels to follow his Captain wherever Valour calls. I follow you without Fear wherever Truth leads the Way.

You appear, anſwered I, to think it a Riddle in Philoſophy that the ſame Bodies ſhould be both attracted and repelled; and indeed there is ſome Reaſon for your thinking ſo. But would not the Riddle be ſtill greater, if I tell you that theſe two contrary Forces, the attractive and repulsive, are of the same Nature, and in short it is only the same Force which discovers itself in different Manners and various Circumstances? The Marchioness at this could scarce forbear laughing. What! said she, do you call the attractive and repulsive Force the same Thing? One acts directly contrary to the other, since the first attracts and the last repels. Are these those sublime Mysteries in Natural Philosophy of which you hardly thought me worthy, and which you have introduced with so much Apparatus? Does not all this greatly resemble the Physician in *Moliere*, who affirmed roast and boil'd to be the same Thing?

What! answered I, do you ridicule the most sacred Things in Natural Philosophy, and of whose Use you are yet ignorant? What a Spirit of Prophaneness still remains in you! But you shall quickly be punished. Remember the Conclusion which you yourself just now deduced from that very Attraction you made so great a Difficulty to admit. Ladies of all Persons have least Reason to to be ſurprized that the ſame Thing ſhould produce contrary Effects. Do not the higheſt Reſerve and an evident Partiality often proceed from the ſame Principle, and teach Connoiſſeurs to draw the ſame Concluſion from them? The Sun hardens and ſoftens according to the different Circumſtances in which he exerciſes his Heat.

This Truth is no leſs evident in the moſt noiſy Affairs of human Life than in the Phænomena of Gallantry and Natural Philoſophy. The ſame Thirſt of leaving an empty Name and Living in the imaginary Breath of Poſterity, burnt the Temple at *Epheſus* in *Aſia*, and precipitated a *Roman* and his Horſe into an open Gulf in the Midſt of the Forum at *Rome*. The ſame Paſſion made *Curtius* an Hero, and *Eroſtratus* an Incendiary.

There are certain Things which to the Vulgar, nay even the philoſophical Vulgar, may appear as evident Contradictions in the ſame Man, whom ſome upon that Account have imagined to be double (as others did the Governor of the Univerſe) ſo then what the one willed the other diſapproved; but are not theſe Contradictions the neceſſary Conſequences of the ſame Paſſion and the ſame Motives?

Thus the very ſame Cauſe, by which Bodies are attracted, may in ſome Circumſtances repel them. There are found certain Analogies between theſe two Forces, which give us great Reaſon to conclude that they are in reality only the ſame Force which produces different Effects.

It is generally found that where the attractive Force is weak, the repulſive too is weak, and where the one is ſtrong, the other is ſtrong alſo. Refraction which depends on one of theſe two Forces, and Reflection on the other, are both effected where there is a Surface that ſeparates two Bodies of different Denſity. For while the Rays proceed in the ſame Medium and do not meet with one of a different Denſity, they are neither reflected nor refracted.

Thoſe Rays which are moſt refrangible,

gible, are likewiſe more eaſily reflected than the reſt. In Bodies by which the Light is more refracted it is likewiſe more ſtrongly reflected. And in general, where the attractive Force is greateſt, the reflective and repulſive is greateſt alſo. Diamonds, which refract the Light very ſtrongly, give it in Proportion a ſtronger Reflection. Hence proceed the Vivacity of their Colours and their fine ſparkling Luſtre.

Theſe Analogies, replied the Marchioneſs, are very pretty and very good, and ſo are the Examples by which you introduced them, and very ſtrongly reproach my Raſhneſs. I am heartily penitent for my Fault in laughing when I ſhould have admired, and deſpiſing what I ought to have regarded with Veneration. But did not you tell me that Reflection happens when Light meets with the ſolid Parts of Bodies and is from thence repelled? This Explication ſeemed very intelligible to me, and perhaps more ſo than what you at preſent intimate.

It is *Des Cartes*, Madam, who gave you

you this Explication, and not I, therefore you may be in ſome Apprehenſions about it. An ingenious Author gives a very uſeful Piece of Advice, that in Philoſophy we ſhould be as diffident of what we imagine ourſelves to underſtand very eaſily, as of what we do not underſtand at all.

If Reflection was made when the Light meets with the ſolid Parts of Bodies (as you ſo clearly underſtand it ought to be) do you know what an Inconvenience would from thence ariſe in Nature, you would no longer have either Toilette or Looking-Glaſſes?

A Surface, however ſmooth and poliſhed it may be, is however full of Protuberances and ſenſible Irregularities diſcoverable by a Microſcope. Imagine all Bodies which you believe the moſt ſmooth and poliſhed, to be like Water when it is rufled by the Wind. The Light muſt be reflected from all Bodies irregularly as it is from Water thus rufled, and could never be ſent back with that Regularity as is neceſſary for you to ſee yourſelf in a a Looking-Glaſs. Is not this paying a great Price for your fine Explication? Is it really true, anſwered ſhe, that it will coſt ſo dear? Perhaps you put me into a greater Terror than the Danger deſerves. Is it not poſſible that theſe Irregularities in the Surfaces of Glaſſes, tho' ſenſible to the Microſcope, may yet be inſenſible to the Light?

You are grown extremely difficult, Madam, anſwered I. The Protuberances and Cavities in the moſt ſmooth and poliſhed Glaſſes are when compared to a Particle of Light, what the *Alps* or *Pyrenees* would be in reſpect of a Tennis-Ball. The Irregularities of a Looking-Glaſs are diſcoverable by common Microſcopes, but there is no Microſcope ſo perfect as to ſhew the Pores of Diamond, through which the Light however paſſes very copiouſly. It would be a terrible Circumſtance for us, if the Particles of Light were not almoſt infinitely ſmall. The Force of Bodies is reckoned from the Quantity of Matter that they contain, which is called the Maſs, and from their Velocity; the greater therefore

therefore their Maſs and Velocity, the greater is their Force.

The Particles of Light have an incredible Velocity, for they come from the Sun to the Earth in about eight Minutes, and thus in eight Minutes they run through a Space of eighty one million Miles. Their Velocity then being ſo extremely great as to exceed more than ten million times that of the ſwifteſt *Engliſh* Horſes, their Maſs muſt be almoſt infinitely ſmall, or elſe a ſingle Particle of Light, inſtead of animating and reviving all Nature by its Appearance, would produce upon our Earth the moſt terrible Effects of a Cannon.

The good Effects, anſwered the Marchioneſs, of that Diffidence we ought to ſhew to Men, extend likewiſe to Philoſophers; for by this Means the one gives greater Proofs of what we deſire ſhould be true, and the other of what really is ſo. I will for the future be very careful not to believe you too haſtily.

For this time at leaſt, anſwered I, you cannot accuſe yourſelf of too much Cre-

Credulity. It will never burthen your Conſcience that you have not had ſufficient Arguments to believe that Reflection is not made by the meeting of Light with the ſolid Parts of Bodies. For beſides the great Inconvenience which would ariſe if this Suppoſition were true, Obſervation informs us, that Light, tranſmitted through a Piece of Glaſs, ſuffers a ſtronger Reflection at going out of the Glaſs than it did at entering into it. Now how is it poſſible that Light ſhould find more ſolid Parts in the Air than in the Glaſs itſelf, to occaſion this ſtronger Reflection?

Beſides, if Water or Oyl be placed immediately behind the Glaſs, the Reflection becomes weaker. Will the Light find fewer ſolid Parts in Water or Oyl than in Air?

Laſtly, if the Air which is behind the Glaſs be taken away by an Inſtrument made for that Purpoſe, the Reflection will be much ſtronger than it was before the Air was removed. Will you ſay that Light meets with a greater Number of ſolid Parts in a Vacuum than in the

the Air? Heaven forbid that I ſhould ſay it, replied the Marchioneſs; I will rather make the repulſive Force to be the Cauſe of Reflection. In theſe Caſes, anſwered I, it is not the repulſive but the attractive Force. When a Ray goes out of the Glaſs into Air, it is attracted by the Air and the Glaſs; hence that Part of it, which was neareſt the Glaſs, returns back as if it had been reflected, if the Air be entirely taken away, this Part being extremely attracted by the Glaſs, and hardly any Thing by what remains after the Air is removed, it returns back again almoſt entire.

But if Water or Oyl (which attract the Ray much more ſtrongly than the Air does) be placed behind the Glaſs, a leſs Part of the Ray will return back than there did while the Air remained. Laſtly, when the Forces of the two Mediums are balanced, as for Inſtance, when a Liquor be applied to the Glaſs of pretty near the ſame Denſity, or another Piece of Glaſs, the Ray muſt paſs entire, and there will be no Reflection.

In general, we may affirm that the attrac-

attractive Force is the Cause of the Reflection of the Rays when the Light, passes from a dense into a rare Medium; and the repulsive, when it passes from a rare to a dense.

In both Cases, since the attractive and repulsive Force are propagated at some Distance from Bodies, the Light is reflected notwithstanding its Distance from the reflecting Body. Just as when it begins to be refracted, it is somewhat distant from the refracting Medium, in the same Manner as it is from the Extremity of Bodies when passing near them, it is turned out of its direct Path and curved by Diffraction. Hence you see that solid Parts and *Des Cartes*'s Explication have less to do with Reflection than ever.

Poor *Des Cartes*, continued she, is attacked in his very last Retrenchments. There is nothing wanting to compleat his Overthrow but for us to assert, that as Light is not reflected from solid Parts, so neither is it transmitted from the Pores of Bodies, and thus he may return back like that momentaneous *Alexander*

of

of the North, who after the most rapid and noisy Victories, at length lost the best of his own Dominions.

In order to deny him every Thing and give him Leave to return home as soon as he pleases, we will at least deny that the Quantity or Magnitude of the Pores in Bodies, contributes any Thing to their Transparency. It is proved on the contrary, that if the Pores of a Body, for Instance Paper, be filled with Water or Oyl, it loses its Opacity and becomes transparent; whereas if the Pores in a Body be multiplied, as when Glass is reduced to Powder, it loses its Transparency and becomes opaque.

It is in Homogeneity we are to seek the Cause of Transparency. If there be many Pores in a Body, and these be filled with a Matter different from that of the Body itself, the Light will meet with a thousand Reflections and Refractions in the internal Parts, so and thus it will be utterly extinguished. The Air ceases to be transparent when it is cloudy, tho' it is then lighter than when it is

clear,

clear, and consequently more porous. Its Opacity can arise from no other Cause but that it is at that Time heterogenous, which makes the Rays that pass through it suffer innumerable Reflections and Refractions, by which Means they are very soon stifled and extinguished. Thus the Froth of Champagne is opaque, tho' much more porous and lighter than the Wine itself.

This seems to furnish us with an Argument to infer, that the Heavens cannot be filled with Matter however rare it be supposed, even if all contained within the vast Orb of *Saturn*, and tho' its Pores should be as small as you can possibly conceive, might, after being perfectly united so as to leave no empty Space, be grasped in one Hand.

What strange Relation is this you tell me? replied the Marchioness. Is the *Newtonian* Philosophy some golden Fleece which we must not undertake the Conquest of, till we have first passed through a thousand strange Portents, and subdued a thousand Monsters of Imagination.

Do

Do you believe, anſwered I, that Gold the precious Subſtance for which Mankind do and ſuffer ſo much, and for which we feel the greateſt Thirſt when we ought to be moſt ſatisfied, Gold I ſay, and Diamonds themſelves, the moſt ſhining Work of Nature, notwithſtanding their great Weight and Gravity, contain a great Quantity of Matter? It will appear ſtrange when I tell you how very little that Quantity really is when compared to that Vacuum between the Parts, and which to our deluded Eye ſeems perfectly full.

The ſolid Parts contained in a Piece of Glaſs are no more conſidered with regard to its Extent, than a Grain of Sand to the terraqueous Globe. It is very ſurprizing how little ſolid Matter there is in the World, and with how few Materials, if I may uſe that Expreſſion, it is built. Perhaps if you knew the Truth you would be afraid you walked upon Cotton, and were in Danger of cruſhing it under your Feet, even if they were as light as thoſe of the ſwift *Camilla*.

Now

Now if the Matter of the Heavens be imagined unconceivably rare and ſubtle, yet the Light which, notwithſtanding its prodigious Velocity, employs according to the laſt Calculations ſix Years in coming from the Stars to us, muſt be intirely extinguiſhed by that Multiplicity of Reflections and Refractions which it muſt ſuffer in that immenſe Paſſage; juſt as a numerous and flouriſhing Army in a long March muſt decreaſe and periſh by the Fatigues and Obſtacles it meets upon the Road.

I ſee with Pleaſure, ſaid the Marchioneſs, how the Properties of our Light conduct us to empty Heaven, and after having ſet the Earth in Motion, to clear its Way. The Diffractions too, anſwered I, which the Light would ſuffer from the Particles of this Celeſtial Matter, would contribute not a little to extinguiſh it, in the ſame Manner as they would do in Bodies that are very porous and heterogeneous. It is ſurprizing that in the Notes which *Perrault* wrote upon *Vitruvius*, he ſeems, if I remember right, to have had ſome faint Notion

of

of this Truth. Rarefaction, said he, (that is, a Distance of Parts) renders Bodies opaque, because these, which were at first homogeneal when rarefied, become heterogeneous.

It seems much more surprizing, said the Marchioness, that any Person could clearly see and demonstrate that two Things so very opposite as Reflection and Refraction should yet arise from the same Cause, This I must confess will always be a Wonder to me.

The Facility, answered I, and the Obstacles which the Light meets in passing out of one Medium into another, are almost in the same Case. Perhaps an exceedingly subtile Fluid diffused in the Confines of the Mediums extremely quick in its Vibrations, and in which the Light by Percussion excites an undulating and tremulous Motion (as a Stone does in Water, or a Voice in the Air) is the Cause of both the Facility and Obstacles in Question. Thus if the Light happens to be in the Concavity of the Waves of this Fluid, it passes freely through it, but if in their

their Summit, it is drove back again.

Hence come the *Fits of easy Transmission and Refraction*, that is, the same Ray of Light is in one Moment transmitted, and in the next reflected; and because the Vibrations of this fluid are exceedingly rapid, the Rays appear to us both transmitted and reflected at the same Time.

But we are now arrived to the Confines of Nature where our Ideas grow dark and confused; these are the Barriers of Knowlege, beyond which no Force of human Faculties is permitted to proceed, I myself perhaps have run too great a Length.

Sir *Isaac Newton* under the Form of Questions proposed many Things which are probably the Recesses where Nature withdraws to conceal herself from mortal Eyes. The Analogy betwixt Sound and Colour, the strange Metamorphoses of Light into Bodies, and Bodies into Light, the two-fold and surprizing Refractions of Island Chrystal, Rock Chrystal, and that Sort lately discovered in *Brasil*, will always be impenetrable

Enig-

Enigmas to Mankind, ſince this OEdipus was not able to ſolve them.

How very different from the modeſt Doubts of this Legiſlator of the Wiſe are the raſh Aſſertions of the Seducers of the Multitude. Theſe however promiſe thoſe very Men, whom they have always deceived with the ſame Flatteries, to open the Temple of Truth ſo often tried in vain, in the moſt expeditious and eaſy Manner by the Help of certain new Principles; juſt as others with certain new Syſtems of their own ſpread artful Nets for human Avarice, and promiſe at once to enrich a Nation which they have always impoveriſhed by the very ſame Schemes. The Pleaſing and vain Deluſion of Hope leads ſome in Haſte to the *Bank*, others to the Academy. The Beginning of an Affair is generally agreeable to our flattering Expectations. The Wind is commonly favourable to the Ship juſt looſed from the Port, and two bright Eyes give an agreeable Invitation at their firſt Appearance. The Bank by converting Hopes at firſt into Gold preſerves

ſerves and increaſes its Reputation, and Philoſophy by judicious Prefaces maintains its Honour, more ſucceſsful in baniſhing old Errors, than ſubſtituting new Truths in their Place. Thus they who by a prudent Diffidence ſoon extricated themſelves from the Snare, either brought back a reputable Increaſe of their Fortune, or were rationally delivered from their paſt Prejudices. But there are very few ſo wiſe as not to loſe the preſent in forming Projects for the future, or not to make the Happineſs of to day, a Step to the Miſery of to-morrow. The Cheat at Length is diſcovered, and the firſt are left with their Scrutoirs, full of Notes worth nothing, while the laſt have their Heads embarraſſed with Notions of Preſſure, *Rotations*, *Globules*, and *Vortices*, the falſe Coin of Philoſophy. Sir *Iſaac Newton*, guided by a ſlow yet ſure Experience, promiſes no more than what Experience is able to perform. Where that leaves him he ſtops, by its Aſſiſtance he diſtinguiſhes Truth from Falſhood, Evidence from Probability, and in the Extent of his *own*, discovers the Limits of the *human* Understanding.

Are not the Rays of Light (says Sir *Isaac Newton)* very small Bodies of different Sizes, the least of which make Violet, the weakest and darkest of all the Colours, and more easily diverted by the attractive Force of the *Prism* from the right Path? And the rest, as they are bigger and bigger, make the stronger and more lucid Colours, Blue, Green, Yellow and Red, and are more difficultly refracted, in Proportion to the greater Strength of the Colours, and the larger Size of the Bodies that compose them?

It is certain that the Rays of Light differ from each other in Colour, Refrangibility, and the Force with which they strike our Senses. Scarlet dazzles the Sight, the Azure of Heaven languidly moves it, and the Verdure of a Meadow strikes it with a very pleasing Sensation.

Only one of these Differences, said the Marchioness, had been sufficient to make an ordinary Philosopher put an absolute Difference in the Size of the Particles of

Light,

Light, whereas two or three are hardly enough to ſupply ours with a Conjecture.

In the vaſt and unlimited Perſpective of Nature (anſwered I) there are Objects that we are for ever condemned to ſee languid and confuſed, without hoping that any Teleſcope can make them appear either leſs diſtant or more diſtinct. The Moderation of our Philoſopher, in never affirming any Thing to be true which was not demonſtrated by Obſervation, may ſerve for an Example to the moſt raſh Aſſerters. Who could have more Reaſon to think himſelf capable of aſcending Heaven, or bringing the Secrets of Nature in Triumph from thence, than Sir *Iſaac Newton*, who, poiſed upon the Wings of *Geometry*, could take his Flight through immenſe Spaces, till then impenetrable to human Curioſity?

What a ſtrange Condition, replied the Marchioneſs, is ours! We know what Size in a Particle at a great Diſtance from our Sight is neceſſary to reflect a certain Colour, but what is this Colour itſelf which we have always immediately before our Eyes? Hardly can we form any Idea of it by a feeble Conjecture: In one Case we have the Sight of a Lynx, in the other we are absolutely blind. There our Senses are refined beyond what we could have expected; here they seem to abandon us all at once.

There are some Persons, answered I, who have believed that the many Difficulties which attend our little Degree of Knowledge, the great Number of Systems, the various Emblems of human Ignorance, and that continual tantalizing which Philosophers suffer in their Searches after Truth, proceed from no other Cause than our want of a sixth natural Sense which might reveal a great Part of what is at present hid from us, and escapes perhaps those five Senses given us by Nature to lay hold on external Objects, and bring them to the Mind.

As there are certain Animals among us, who, by virtue of Senses, of which we perhaps have no Knowledge, foresee the Change of the Seasons, and approach of the Morning, and, without having read *Dioscorides* or any other Botanist, can amidst a thousand others distinguish that salutary Herb that cures theirHurts, who knows but in some other System, (in theWorld of *Jupiter* perhaps,) there may be Animals which, more sharp-sighted than our Philosophers, may discover the Size of those Particles that compose the Variety of Colours, and in what manner, without the Assistance of Ropes or Pullies,they may attract *Saturn* at a Distance of more than three hundred and fifty Millions of Miles?

But in return, as in that Planet, which is not depopulated by the Race of War, the Inhabitants have no Idea of the Pleasures of Love, so, according to the agreeable Historian of these Worlds, every Thing is diversified, and put in a just Balance; those People who are throughly acquainted with the Nature of Colours, may perhaps want the Sense proper to give them a Perception of the most agreeable Harmony of those Colours upon the Cheeks of their *Chloes*, and tho' perfectly skilled in the Attractions of the Planets, are perhaps insensible to the more pleasing Attractions of Beauty, which are preferable to any Speculation whatever.

But however it be with regard to our present Speculation, the most vain perhaps of all others, it is not for our Advantage to seek Occasions to put us in Mind of our Defects, nor be so ingenious in tormenting ourselves. We shall not be destitute of either Knowledge or Pleasure, if we make a good Use of the Senses fallen to our Lot. Though you know nothing wherein consists the Nature of Light and Colours but by Conjecture, there will not perhaps be wanting some Persons to affirm you know much more of it than is proper for a Lady. The Fault will be thrown entirely upon Me, who upon those few Verses which gave Occasion to our Subject, have made you a Comment, long enough for a Poem upon the *Newtonian* Philosophy. It will be well for it, if you dissemble your Knowledge with those Persons who ridicule what they ought to learn, and if to the Science of Natural Philosophy you join that of the World.

What,

What, cried the Marchioneſs, am I ſo learned that I ought to ſtudy to be ignorant? May I venture ſeriouſly to call myſelf a *Newtonian*? You have already renounced your philoſophical Errors, anſwered I. The Light of *Newtonianiſm* has diſſipated the *Carteſian* Phantoms which deluded your Sight. You are now really a *Newtonian*, and it is no ſmall Advantage to *Truth* that you are ſo. I will ſome time give a Hiſtory of the fine Conqueſt I have acquired for Her, and I am certain if I could give a juſt Deſcription of my fair Diſciple, my Book would never want Readers, nor true Philoſophy a numerous Train of Proſelytes. You ſhall be the *Venus* that muſt lend the agreeable Ceſtus to this auſtere *Juno*, and give her thoſe attractive Charms that will render her engaging and amiable to Mankind.

FINIS.

CPSIA information can be obtained
at www.ICGtesting.com
Printed in the USA
BVHW041243030619
550004BV00005B/291/P

9 780343 317508